Unravelling Racing

A Guide

Lionel Beecroft

200th Derby Roll Call
Roy Miller

The most famous race in the world

Published by Lambee Publications
Dearnley House, Elsted, West Sussex. GU29 0JT
Tel:01730 813233
E-mail: lionelbeecroft@yahoo.co.uk

First Edition 2008

© Lionel Beecroft

ISBN: 978-0-904775-60-0

Printed by G. H. Smith & Son
Market Place, Easingwold, York. YO61 3AB
Tel: 01347 821329
E-mail: info@ghsmith.com

Illustrations by Roy Miller
Tel: 01332 356874

Contents

	Page
Foreword	4
Introduction	5
Obstacles to understanding	8
Establishing the merit of a horse: **form**	14
Establishing the merit of a horse: **speed**	36
Other factors influencing race results: **race variables**	42
Pulling it all together: selection and decision making process	54
Conclusion	64
Glossary of terms	65
Appendix	70
Acknowledgements	72

Foreword

This book is a gem.

Lionel Beecroft fell in love with horse racing as a schoolboy when his father took him to York Races for the traditional Ebor meeting. The excitement created then by the colourful, exuberant and thrilling spectacle has never left him. A successful racehorse owner – his Astrac won the Wokingham Stakes at Royal Ascot in 1995 ridden by Seb Sanders, now joint Champion Jockey. He has a wealth of knowledge and experience to pass on to the reader.

The Author shows us a clearly defined and logically explained process to assist in solving the puzzle that is presented to all race goers – namely what will win the race? In so doing he throws light on many aspects of British Horse racing and the result is a narrative which is not only informative, but also both interesting and entertaining.

Especially valuable to anyone relatively new to racing; this book will also appeal to all lovers of sport on the Turf.

Michael Gibbs
Worthing
September 2008

INTRODUCTION

'Nec te nobelium fugiat certamen equorum'
(Never miss a good race meeting)
Ovid

I am often shocked and amazed, when I go to the races, at the behaviour of my friends. They invest their hard-earned cash on horses using the craziest criteria for selection. They seem to think that the colour of the jockey's shirt, the number on the saddlecloth or the nag's name has some bearing on a horse's athletic ability. If they do use some science or logic it appears to be made up on the spur of the moment and discarded just as quickly. Failing all else they throw themselves upon the mercy of a chap they met at the bar who has heard from so-and-so that Bounding Bertie in the 3:30 is a nailed on cert! This sort of behaviour tells me that many people take a superficial view of the sport because it is hard to access, hard to get to grips with. Indeed there seem to be many perceived obstacles to gaining a better understanding.

My working hypothesis is that the result of most horse races can be predicted. These outcomes can be determined by carefully assessing the relative merits of the animals participating and by trying to understand the probable influence of a small number of specific factors that can affect a horse's race performance either in a positive or negative way. Factors such as the going, the distance, the track etc., can affect how well a horse runs its race. Therefore with the correct data and some rigorous analysis it is possible to find the main two or three contenders and hopefully the winner of any given race. Where you tend to fail is when there is insufficient performance data on all or some of the participants, which is mainly in races for two and three year olds. Or where there is very little difference in merit between several of the runners thus making the result difficult to call. And, of course, where daft selection criteria are used.

This assertion, that the result of many races is predictable, may surprise you because most games, sports or pastimes that involve betting are subject to huge amounts of chance and the results are random and unfathomable. For example anything involving dice, cards or little spinning balls are mostly games of pure chance and can seriously affect your wealth. Casinos are the purveyors of such games of chance and many are open 24/7; they also spin the wheel, throw the dice or turn the cards every couple of minutes. With such an avalanche of betting opportunities and with all the odds stacked heavily against the player by the house and the nature of the game, how can you hope to win? With some other sports such as football, boxing or golf the results are so predictable that the odds available are miserly and consequently subsidiary betting, normally spread betting, takes place on the margin of victory or defeat. Very dangerous with the complicated multipliers used, as you cannot work out how much you are down to win or lose in advance.

Compare and contrast with horse racing; there are only 6 or 7 races on each card and your chances are commensurate with the quality of your analysis. Application wedded to research and understanding can help you locate the winner (and usually at interesting odds). Skill and judgement are very necessary attributes for the player. They are certainly required because the quantity of information available on the merit of each horse and its capacity to cope with track vagaries and other variables in a race is huge. It is often quite raw data and sometimes complex; there is also lots of irrelevant stuff too that needs discarding or ignoring. Therefore, to the novice or beginner, it can be a daunting task, first to locate the data and an even bigger one to then sort and arrange it in order to make some practical use out of it. I can fully understand why some trivialise racing and the selection process or abandon it to the hacks, tipsters and the mad enthusiasts who they then rely on for guidance.

The data for each race is available and awaiting critical scrutiny if someone is willing and able to do it: to locate the evidence like a detective, prepare and present it like a barrister, sum it up like a judge, make decisions like a jury and then come to a clear conclusion based on the known evidence. The whole process should be interesting and fun.

So shun systems, they are bookmaker's friends. Desist from trying to seek out 'inside information' it is generally unreliable. Rely instead on yourself, your own reasoning and analysis of the evidence you can gather on a horse, its ability and racing characteristics. Dick Whitford, one of the founders of *Timeform,* who produced the first universal handicap based on form, said when reflecting on what he had learned after researching the project and constructing the handicap:

'Racehorses are figurable; not approximately or roughly, but almost exactly…
So much so that I had to keep reminding myself that I was dealing not so much with numbers but with flesh and blood living creatures.'

Indeed!

If you wish to get more enjoyment out of the sport and try to improve your win to bet ratio it is essential to understand how to:

- **Judge** or establish the real **merit** or ability of a horse
- **Identify** the **variable factors** that can affect a horse's performance in a given race
- **Locate** the necessary **data**
- **Analyse** that data **to predict** the result

Plus of course you need to have sufficient knowledge of the relevant background information that provides context and can assist interpretation and understanding of the above. Factors such as breeding, handicapping, rules of racing, topography of courses, racing jargon etc; will help you better synthesise the data.

Racing is a data-rich sport. The more informed you are the better your chance of winning, so turning data into information is a large and interesting challenge. This book will help you:

- Locate the main data sources (on each horse, its record and racing characteristics)
- Turn data into information
- Assess and analyse the information created
- Understand the relevant background information of horse racing to provide context
- Apply the hints and tips on selection and betting strategies suggested

It is for this reason that I wrote this book. To help the enthusiastic or novice race goer gain a better understanding of the game, add a little more structure to their selection method and in the process, open up the glorious spectacle and the excitement that is to be found in horse racing. And hopefully, as with Ovid, you will never miss a good race meeting and get much more enjoyment, interest and profit out of it to boot.

Good luck!

**The Betting Post
Thomas Rowlandson
(Mansell Collection)**

Betting has always been an integral part of the racing scene

Chapter One

Obstacles to Understanding

'I went to the racetrack today; it was closed, so I shoved all my money through the letterbox'
W.C. Fields

The quote at the head of this chapter, as well as being quite droll, also gives us a few valuable insights into the world of horse racing. It implies that:

- Horse racing has a unique fascination and compulsion
- Money and betting are involved
- It is almost impossible to beat the bookie

I cannot but concur with the first two points but I would very strongly disagree with the third. As I mentioned earlier, it is entirely possible to beat the bookie but you have to set about the task in a methodical and logical way, armed with the relevant information. In addition, you must also prime yourself with a great deal of self-control and discipline to bet only on the races that throw up the necessary data concerning each and every horse participating.

It seems to me that a large number of curious, intelligent people wager their hard-earned lucre on horses using the daftest selection criteria, or participate vicariously by following tipsters. Actually, I don't mind so much people using daft criteria if they decide they can't fathom a particular race and just want to have a bit of fun and a flutter. It does trouble me when they rely heavily on tipsters for it means they are applying little or no judgement and are probably not trying to understand what is going on; they have given up. This is a tragedy for there is nothing more fascinating and satisfying than to see the main contenders present themselves as you analyse the essential characteristics of the runners in a given race. Please do not surrender this important facet of your involvement in racing to the hacks and tipsters.

Why do so many punters lose their reason or faculty for judgement at the turnstile or when they turn to the racing page of their daily newspaper? I would venture that there are a number of contributory factors. There are several obstacles to better understanding and enjoying the sport. It is worth examining the main ones if only to realise they are not as daunting as they first seem and can be easily surmounted.

Problem One: Information and Presentation

When you go racing you have a number of interesting puzzles to solve in order to find the winner of each race. There are two approaches you can take:

a) Make a guess, use a pin, pick a nice name, select a lucky number, choose a pretty colour etc., etc., and trust to providence.

b) Analyse the available information (each horse's form and its racing characteristics) and make an informed decision.

I would imagine most people would elect to go down route b), however one of the biggest problems, in your quest to find the winner, is that the information presented on the racing page of your daily newspaper or even on your race card at the track, is regrettably not comprehensive enough to provide you with the information you require to make an informed decision or even an educated guess. Set out below is the information you are usually presented with in the newspaper and which alarmingly most people rely on at the races or when having a flutter with the high street bookie.

2.05 ATALANTA STKS (LISTED) (CLASS 1) 1m £22,708	
1 226 BARSHIBA (27)(D) D Elsworth 4 9 0	T Quinn 10
2 215 IN THE LIGHT (17)(D)(BF) Sir M Stoute 4 9 0	J Fortune 11
3 640 NEARDOWN BEAUTY (9)(D) A McCabe 5 9 0	Doubtful 2
4 1-0 QUE PIENSA CAT (ARG)(27) S bin Suroor 4 9 0	L Dettori 5
5 054 SELINKA [V] (17)(CD) R Hannon 4 9 0	R Hughes 7
6 100 RAYMI COYA (CAN)(27)(D) M Botti 3 8 12	T Durcan 12
7 051 ROSALEEN (56)(CD) B Meehan 3 8 12	A Munro 4
8 -14 ADA RIVER (106)(D) A Balding 3 8 8	W Buick 3
9 022 EVA'S REQUEST (13) M Channon 3 8 8	E Creighton 13
10 165 GHAIDAA (31)(BF) M Jarvis 3 8 8	M Dwyer 1
11 211 LINDELAAN [B] (42)(D) Sir M Stoute 3 8 8	R L Moore 8
12 342 MEKONG MELODY (12)(D) C Cox 3 8 8	P Robinson 9
13 353 SHABIBA (29) M Tregoning 3 8 8	R Hills 6
S.P. F'CAST: 4-1 Lindelaan, 5-1 Barshiba, 11-2 In The Light, 7-1 Selinka, 8-1 Eva's Request, 10-1 Rosaleen, Raymi Coya, 12-1 others.	

Is there enough data on this card to enable a sensible selection?
Even the beginner would realise that there is nothing here to help them differentiate between horses!

Here is a quick audit of what is generally found in your paper and what is missing:

Data Provided
Time of race
Distance
Names of runners
Age
Weight to be carried
Draw
Days since last run
Form: last 5 outings
Trainer
Jockey
Going

Data Missing
Current handicap mark?
Changes to handicap mark last 5 runs?
At what handicap mark were the previous wins achieved?
Going for last 5 runs?
On what going were the previous wins?
Have last 5 runs been on same surface? (all weather/turf)
Speedfigure for last run plus best speedfigure (including going and distance)?
Stepping up or down in class?
On which track(s) were previous win(s)?
Rider last 5 runs + wins?
Sex of runners

A glance at the above chart tells us that there is at least as much relevant data missing as presented!

Trying to solve the riddle presented by each race is fun, but it is more fun and less frustrating when you have all the appropriate information you need to complete the task to your satisfaction. Lacking the necessary data to make an informed decision can throw people on the mercy of the tipsters. This is just as bad. Consider the following tipsters table, which is not untypical:

Tipsters Table for the Stewards' Cup, 3:50 Goodwood, Saturday, 2nd August 2008

Publication	Selection
Racing Post	Prime Defender
Times	Prime Defender
Telegraph	Buachaill Dona
Guardian	Off The Record
Independent	Machinst
Mail	Borderlescot
Express	Something
Mirror	Knot in Wood
Sun	Prime Defender
Star	Sohraab

**If you thought picking a horse was bad enough try picking a tipster!
Ten tipsters and eight different horses; and the winner was Conquest!**

So for rigorous race analysis the information given in most daily papers is very, very basic and incomplete and has to be supplemented from other sources. In the following chapters I will show you what data you need to solve the puzzle of each race and how to understand or interpret the form of each horse and its racing characteristics (particularly its preferences and dislikes of the factors that can affect its race performance). Part of this exercise will also be to highlight where this important supplementary data can be found. Then you will be much better able to differentiate between the horses in each race.

Problem Two: Interest Groups

I could never understand why there was so much contradiction amongst the 'experts' in racing till it dawned on me that racing is served by many different interest groups whose objectives are not always complementary or aligned. For example: The Jockey Club, The British Horseracing Authority, The Owners Association, The Breeders, The Bookies, The Racecourses, The Trainers Association, The Jockeys Association, The Racing Press, etc., etc.; can each put a different spin on important information or data which can sometimes confuse the unwary or uninitiated. Racing politics can be quite divisive. For example, the Labour Party in its last 2 manifestoes undertook to sell *The Tote* to racing (The BHA and its associate bodies). The Government appointed not one, not two, but three advisors to assist it. The negotiations have dragged on for many, many months; the Government has rejected two bids and are now threatening to sell *The Tote* to the bookies. Each side blames the other; the advisors still get paid very well. This is a crisis for British Racing, the tenth largest industry in the UK. Who is at fault?

Here are a couple of other examples from the archives to demonstrate that facts, events or opinions are never as clear cut as we would like and open to (quite a lot of) interpretation. Here names have been changed or omitted to protect the innocent.

Example: A promising three year old much fancied for the Derby. To date he has only run as far as a mile (with much credit) and is unproven over further. His ante post price is shortening for the Blue Ribbon event. The Racing Press have a view that due to his breeding and style of racing he is unlikely to stay a mile and a half. The owner insists he will, the trainer (who co-incidentally has other Derby entries) is more enigmatic stating that 'he is a good horse and I have every confidence in his ability'. No jockey has yet been booked to ride but views amongst the riding fraternity appear mixed! Who do you believe? Or do you have an opinion?

Example: Most recently the times for a couple of races on the card at a top track were exceptional, several horses putting up their best ever speedfigures. Some sections of the industry press felt that the times posted were suspect. Allegedly the running rail had been moved prior to the day's racing to protect some of the ground thus shortening the distance of the suspect races. The racecourse confirmed that the running rail had been moved but maintained that it did not much affect the distance but may have presented slightly better ground. Some of the jockeys involved insist that their horses produced performances of true merit. Who or what would you believe? Would you treat the times with caution?

I hope these examples illustrate that sometimes there can be a great deal of ambiguity in racing and it is therefore always better to be well informed, to have an opinion and a point of view, to make your own judgements and not rely on the 'experts'. Or, at least, to understand where they are coming from. You may be right, you may be wrong but if you have considered the facts and made a decision based on what **you** know it's probably as good as anybody's.

Trust yourself; stay informed, have an opinion!

Problem Three: Language

My father called it 'parlance of the trade' and every one has one. Different professions always cloak their industry in a special language or jargon to retain some mystique or authority. Racing is no different, probably worse, because you have several different constituencies or trades whose code you have to try to break.

Alas, we cannot legislate to have the different tribes in racing speak clear, intelligible English that we can all understand. The only solution is to go native and try to comprehend their patois, and to this end I have included a glossary of terms and phrases at the back of the book. A quick dip into it from time to time, a bit of practice and in no time you will be able to hold a basic conversation in racing speak.

Problem Four: Social

Racing is often known as the Sport of Kings. This is because, until most recently, many owners were royalty, aristocracy, very well bred or very well heeled. Even in these more egalitarian times it still appears to be a fairly socially exclusive pastime. It does not help when you go to the racecourse and find different 'enclosures' for the paying customer; the Silver Ring, Tattersalls and Members. Plus of course the temporary marquees for special guests, private boxes and separate seating areas for members of the Jockey Club, stewards and the rest of the smart set. These various compounds have the look and feel of social segregation, particularly heightened by the notices advising of strict dress codes in practice and warning signs of exclusion zones for the unbadged and uninitiated. Ascot, even out of Royal Week, can be quite intimidating with the bowler-hatted attendants checking your attire and credentials.

Even a glance at your race card can make you feel out of place and like a lowly piece of cheese, especially when you read the names of the Stewards officiating. With *Viscount **This**, The Right Honourable **That*** and *Lady **The Other*** featured in the line-up it usually reads like *Debretts* or *Who's Who* and doesn't really strike me as being a fairly good representative cross section of British Society! Clearly only belted earls or their aristocratic cousins can understand the rules of racing and be trusted, unlike the rest of us, to make sensible judgements on the running of a race. However this part of racing is still policed by the Jockey Club, who are a self-elected body. Their rules for membership are particularly hard to satisfy; you have to be an aristocrat, an old Etonian or of similar ilk. Oh, and I forgot to mention, you can't apply to join the club; you have to be invited.

To their credit the Racecourses and the Jockey Club, egged on by the Racehorse Owners Association, are endeavouring to become more 'customer friendly' and over the last few years have made great strides in making the punter feel more welcome and the whole racing package much more pleasant and enjoyable. The **'Don't Do'** and **'Keep Out'** signs have started coming down, some of the barmier dress codes have been relaxed and there has been an outbreak of crèches at most courses and even smiling amongst the formerly grim-faced attendants. I'm sure all of these initiatives will make racing much more customer and family friendly and no doubt will help attract more visitors. However it is the people, the racing fraternity, combined with the horses and the spectacle that makes the whole experience exhilarating and fun.

Racing can be a dangerous and uncertain career or livelihood for those involved. Race riding is fraught with dangers and many jockeys have the scars to prove it. Training horses is beset by uncertainty and by factors often out of the control of any guiding hand or influence. Horses being flesh and blood can break down, catch viruses or be downright temperamental. The punter too must learn to be sanguine in the face of frequent disappointment. Winning hopes can frequently be dashed by cruel circumstances entirely beyond their control. Fortune can fluctuate quickly and often in racing; one minute you are up, the next you are down. I'm sure it is for these reasons that racing people are full of fun, because people who regularly have to face danger and uncertainty either have to laugh and joke about it and live for the moment or become anxious, miserable, grumbling introverts.

Indeed most racing people are generous, gregarious, welcoming and entirely inclusive and revel in the moment. If you want an afternoon of light-hearted fun and enjoyment, sometimes in the company of complete strangers, then the racecourse is the best place. Phil Bull, the racing genius, called it the great triviality; it's meant to be fun, a diversion from the daily grind and most definitely not to be taken too seriously.

Royal Ascot Ladies Day
Roy Miller

Royal Ascot week is probably the best racing on offer anywhere in Europe. However some people see it as a way to show off their smart new frock or waistcoat!

Chapter Two

Establishing the Merit of a Horse

Form

**'A man's past is known as history; a woman's history is known as her past,
but a horse's past is described as form'**
Anon

Form: the previous record of a horse, athlete, etc. especially with regard to fitness.
(Collins Dictionary)

Over the last 400 years or so the combined genius of The British Horse Racing Establishment has produced:

- The Thoroughbred Racehorse
- A global breeding industry worth billions
- A system for rating and ranking racehorses (handicapping)
- Rules for the organisation and conduct of Racing
- The attendant supporting bodies: Bookmakers, The Tote, (Pari-Mutuel) The Racing Press, Commercial Breeders, Bloodstock Agents, Trainers etc.

Establishing a process for ranking and rating horses was central to these significant developments. So before examining form in more detail let's take a quick look at the following:

The Thoroughbred Racehorse
The Breed
The Development of organised racing
A System for rating and ranking horses

This will provide some useful context as well as help us understand why developing a rating system was so important and why form, or a horse's racing record, is important in establishing merit.

The Thoroughbred Racehorse

The thoroughbred racehorse comes in all shapes, sizes and colours. They can be as small as 15 and as large as 17 hands and on average weigh from about 950 to 1000lb. Most are bay, brown, (dark brown almost black) chestnut or grey; however some less common colours include roan and palomino. The face and lower legs may be marked with white but white will generally not appear on the body. Thoroughbreds are athletic in appearance with a well-defined head on a long neck, high withers, a deep chest, a good depth of hindquarters and long legs. They are agile, very speedy, spirited and bold. Northern Dancer was regarded as one of the best racehorses of the 20th century, as shown in the picture of him on the next page. All horses should aspire to this athletic ideal.

Northern Dancer
Roy Miller

Not only was he a world class racehorse, but also a world class sire too

The Breed

In 1688 the **Byerly Turk**, the first of the famous three Arab stallions from which over 90% of today's thoroughbreds are descended, was brought to this country by Captain Robert Byerly to stand at Goldsborough Hall, Knaresborough, Yorkshire. The other two, the **Darley Arabian**, and the **Godolphin Arabian**, were imported shortly afterwards in 1704 and 1729 respectively. They were bred with the native 'hobbies' and running horses and this, over time, produced or created the thoroughbred racehorse. The hobbies and running horses provided the speed and the imported Arabs and Turks provided the stamina for which the thoroughbred is noted. *The General Stud Book*, in which every thoroughbred's pedigree can be traced, was first published in 1791 by James Weatherby of Newmarket. He sought to establish the pedigree of all subsequent English Thoroughbred horses and laid the foundation of studbooks around the globe, which are the basis of the present international horse racing industry.

The Development of Organised Racing

Early History: As long as men have been about they have been racing horses; The Ancient Greeks, The Romans, The Mongols and even The Ancient Britons were at it. Early records show that in 12th century England races were held in Chester and at Smithfield on public holidays. However it was not until the late 17th century that racing, as we know it, started to get organised.

Around this time there were a number of separate but important events that led to the development of the breed and equally important, the organisation and conduct of thoroughbred racing:

Headquarters: In the early 17th century James I built a country retreat near Newmarket, then an obscure village, and so began the development of the town as a racing centre. He was not a keen racing man but his courtiers were. The first recorded match on Newmarket Heath was in 1622 between horses of Lord Salisbury and the Marquis of Buckingham. The racecourse was officially opened in 1636 during Charles I's reign. Charles II, after his restoration in 1666, continued the royal link with Newmarket, founding a series of races there known as Royal Plates and actually competed in some of them. This continuation of royal patronage helped Newmarket develop as the headquarters of British Racing.

Rules of Racing: In the middle of the eighteenth century *The Jockey Club* was founded to give leadership and substance to the organisation and conduct of horse racing. Indeed racing became the first-ever regulated sport in Britain.

Records: In 1727 John Cheny's matchbook provided a central record for results and was a forerunner of James Weatherby's Racing Calendar.

Racecourses: By 1800 there were 83 racing tracks established in Britain for racing 'under rules'. Regrettably, over the last 200 years some have disappeared like Lincoln, Hurst Park, Alexander Palace and Manchester.

Establishing the relative merits of all horses racing or *Handicapping:* Admiral Henry Rous published his book *'The Laws and Practice of Horse Racing'* in 1850 which introduced the concept and the practical logistics of handicapping and his weight-for-age scale, all of which remain largely intact today.

No doubt all these horses are of differing ability!

So how are they assessed, rated and graded according to merit?

Read On!

**As suggested by the title of this picture both Admiral Rous and George Payne did much to put
in place the organisation and structures to make racing what it is today**

A system for rating and ranking horses:

All these events were important in establishing the breed and the organisational structure to support racing. However it was Admiral Rous and his handicapping system that began to develop an accepted, standard process for rating and ranking horses.

Here are four simple questions regarding ratings and the handicap:

> *Why rate horses?*
> *What does a horse do with its rating or handicap mark when it's got one?*
> *How does a horse go about getting a handicap mark?*
> *How does the handicapping system work in practise?*

In the rest of this chapter I will try to answer these questions in turn and by doing so I hope to show, not only how important Admiral Rous' innovation was, but also to highlight the main types of race in the UK and explain how the handicapping or form rating system works in practice.

Q1 Why rate horses?

Horses, of course, vary enormously in athletic ability and in order to make any sporting contest between them interesting and competitive it is necessary to rank and band them to ensure those of similar ability compete against each other. Before Admiral Rous' innovation it was the owner or trainer who did any assessment of merit in a non standard and un-scientific way. But with no detailed and accepted method of assessing merit, and with no banding of races, the poor horses had to run several heats a day to prove their class in order to qualify for races. Poor buggers! So Admiral Rous created a significant breakthrough with his new and efficient handicapping system.

Today The British Horseracing Authority (BHA), the body that organises and regulates the sport, has the official task of rating the animals. It employs a team of handicappers whose job it is to observe each and every horse in their races, note their performance and encapsulate or express their ability in a number. After each race a horse's rating is reviewed; it can go up, down or remain the same depending upon the performance. It's totally fluid and dynamic. At one end of the scale, that expresses a horse's ability, you have really exceptional horses like Shergar, Dancing Brave, Brigadier Gerard, Nijinsky and Mill Reef who were rated in the mid to high 130's. Normally the best or Group One horses are rated in the high 120's. At the other end of the merit scale you have the Dobbins, Longfaces and Slowcoaches; poor horses of little talent who nobody has ever heard and who are rated in the low 30's or below. The average rating of a horse on the flat is 59. Like many things in life these ratings follow the normal distribution pattern or bell-shaped curve. You will find a few at either end of the scale with the bulk of the population spread across the middle. This numeric rating goes under different names and aliases. It is called variously; the BHA rating, the official rating, the form rating or the handicap mark. All these are used interchangeably. Henceforward I shall refer to it as the rating, the form rating or the handicap mark:

The normal distribution of BHA ratings:					
130	**120+**	**90**	**59**	**40**	**0**
Super Horse	Group 1 Horse	Good Handicapper	Average Rating	Poor Handicapper	Dud

**Dancing Brave and Pat Eddery at Longchamp
Roy Miller**

Dancing Brave was one of the outstanding horses of the twentieth century

Q2 What does a horse do with its rating or handicap mark when it's got one?

A horse's official rating is its entry ticket to different types and classes of race; the higher the rating the better the horse and the better the class of race it can enter (and better prize money and more prestige). Therefore the rating indicates not only the ability of the horse but also the quality of the race in which it can participate. Basically there are 2 types of race, **Group** and **Handicap**; and there are different grades within each of these race types.

Group Races (Class 1): The great divide occurs at a rating of 110. At 110+ a horse participates in Group Races or Class 1 races. There are four grades to these Class 1 races and they are, in ascending order of importance and quality; Listed, Group 3, Group 2 and Group 1 races. The

Derby and the Prix de l' Arc de Triomphe are well known examples of Group 1 races. In all class 1 races horses compete on ability alone and carry the same weight *except* for age and sex allowances and weight penalties for previous wins in this grade of race. Here are some examples of the allowances and conditions set out for each grade of these Class 1 races to demonstrate how they work in practice. If you read the conditions and then take a closer look at the runners it is fairly easy to assess how they work.

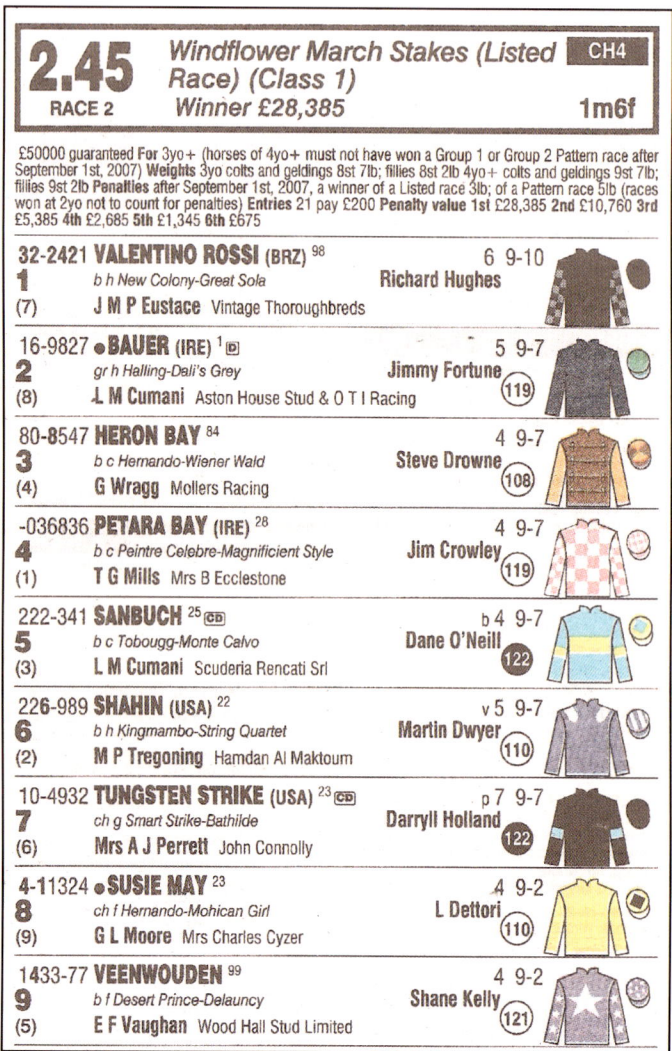

Note all horses carry the same weight **except** 3 year olds who get a weight allowance from older horses and the fillies get a weight allowance from the colts. In this race there are also weight penalties for wins in other Group or Listed races. **Valentino Rossi** (9st.10lb) is carrying a 3lb penalty for winning a listed race. **Susie May** and **Veenwouden** are receiving a 5lb sex allowance from the colts and geldings.

<table>
<tr><td>

2.40
RACE 3

</td><td>

CGA Geoffrey Freer Stakes
(Group 3) (Class 1)
Winner £36,900.50

</td><td>CH4</td></tr>
</table>

2.40 RACE 3 — *CGA Geoffrey Freer Stakes (Group 3) (Class 1)* — *Winner £36,900.50* — (1m5f61y)1m5½f — CH4

£65000 guaranteed **For** 3yo+ **Weights** 3yo colts and geldings 8st 6lb; fillies 8st 3lb 4yo+ colts and geldings 9st 3lb; fillies 9st **Penalties** after September 1st, 2007, a winner of a Group 3 race of 1m4f or more 2lb; of a Group 2 race of 1m4f or more 4lb; of a Group 1 race of 1m4f or more 6lb (races won at 2yo not to count for penalties) (for the purposes of this race, races in excess of 1m 3f 110yds and in excess of 2310m will count as races of 1m4f). **Weight for age** 3 from 4yo+ 11lb **Entries** 20 pay £310 **Penalty value 1st** £36,900.50 **2nd** £13,988 **3rd** £7,000.50 **4th** £3,490.50 **5th** £1,748.50 **6th** £877.50

3.15 RACE 3 — *totesport.com Celebration Mile (Group 2) (Class 1)* — *Winner £56,770* — 1m — CH4

£100000 guaranteed **For** 3yo+ **Weights** 3yo colts and geldings 8st 9lb; fillies 8st 6lb; 4yo+ colts and geldings 9st 1lb; fillies 8st 12lb **Penalties** after September 1st, 2007, a winner of a Group 2 race 3lb; of a Group 1 race 6lb (races won at 2yo not to count for penalties) **Weight for age** 3 from 4yo+ 6lb **Entries** 60 pay £150 **1st Forfeit** 37 pay £300 **Confirmed** 10 pay £150 **Penalty value 1st** £56,770 **2nd** £21,520 **3rd** £10,770 **4th** £5,370 **5th** £2,690

1 (2)	11-1152 **BANKABLE** (IRE) 35 CD BF / b c Medicean-Dance To The Top / L M Cumani Ronchalon Racing (UK) Ltd	4 9-1 Dane O'Neill (132)	
2 (3)	26-4420 **DOCOFTHEBAY** (IRE) 64 CD BF / ch c Docksider-Baize / J A Osborne Paul J Dixon	b 4 9-1 Shane Kelly (126)	
3 (1)	4780433 **DUBAI'S TOUCH** 22 CD / b c Dr Fong-Noble Peregrine / M Johnston Salem Suhail	4 9-1 Darryll Holland (122)	
4 (5)	11-2115 •**THIRD SET** (IRE) 9 CD BF / b g Royal Applause-Khamseh / Saeed Bin Suroor Godolphin	5 9-1 L Dettori (127)	
5 (4)	3-24222 **RAVEN'S PASS** (USA) 24 / ch c Elusive Quality-Ascutney / J H M Gosden Stonerside Stable Llc	3 8-9 Jimmy Fortune (138)	

For this Group 2 race 3-year-old colts carry 8st.9lb, fillies 8st.6lb. Older horses carry 9st.1lb for colts and geldings and 8st.12lb fillies. None of these runners is carrying a penalty. **Raven's Pass** gets an age allowance of 6lb, being a three-year-old.

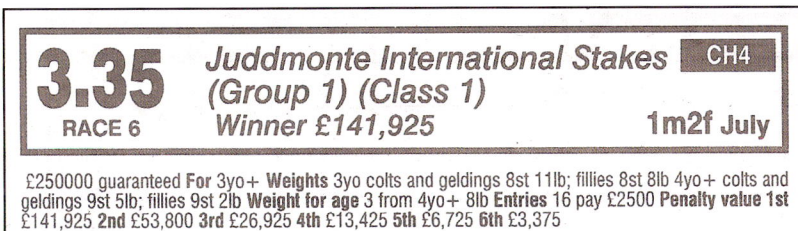

3.35 RACE 6 — *Juddmonte International Stakes (Group 1) (Class 1)* — *Winner £141,925* — 1m2f July — CH4

£250000 guaranteed **For** 3yo+ **Weights** 3yo colts and geldings 8st 11lb; fillies 8st 8lb 4yo+ colts and geldings 9st 5lb; fillies 9st 2lb **Weight for age** 3 from 4yo+ 8lb **Entries** 16 pay £2500 **Penalty value 1st** £141,925 **2nd** £53,800 **3rd** £26,925 **4th** £13,425 **5th** £6,725 **6th** £3,375

Note: as Group One races are the very pinnacle of racing there are no penalties for winning other races, even Group 1.

Handicap Races (Class 2 to 7): If a horse is rated less than 110 then it competes in handicap races. The majority of all races in the UK are handicaps. In these races each horse carries a different weight, which is dictated by its BHA rating; the higher the rating the higher the weight to be carried. This weight differential is in place to equalise the chances of winning for all horses participating. By giving each horse an equal chance, the argument goes, more emphasis is placed on a horse performing to its potential within a race. The handicap therefore penalises merit in order to make these races more competitive, better mediums for betting and to heighten the excitement and entertainment factor. Each time a horse wins or runs well it is re-rated upwards which means it must carry more weight in its next race. If its rating goes up 3 or 5 points then it will carry 3 or 5lb more in its next race. If a horse doesn't finish in the first 3 or 4 it will probably be re-rated downwards by perhaps 1 or 2 points so the next time it runs it will carry 1 or 2lb less. The horse's form rating should be a reflection of its past performances and also of its current ability.

A horse might run up a sequence of two or three handicap race wins, with the weight to be carried upped after each run. However there will come a time when the weight handicap catches up with the horse and it can no longer win. Then it has to keep running, without success, in order to bring its mark and weight back to a winning level.

There are 6 classes or grades of handicap races:

Class 2 for horses rated 86 to 110
Class 3 for horses rated 76 to 95
Class 4 for horses rated 66 to 85
Class 5 for horses rated 56 to 75
Class 6 for horses rated 46 to 55
Class 7 for horses rated 0 to 45

For example, in a Class 2 race, open to horses rated 86 to 110, any horse rated 110 would carry the top weight allotted. A horse rated 109 would carry 1lb less and so on down the handicap to a horse rated 86 who would be carrying 24lb less than the top weighted horse. In theory 1lb or 1 point is supposed to be equal to 1 length at the end of a 12-furlong race and if the handicapping system worked perfectly all the horses participating would cross the finish line together.

This, of course, never happens because the system isn't 100% perfect; it's more approximate than accurate. Each horse is different and the handicap and prevailing race conditions will not affect them all uniformly. Such races, therefore, open up possibilities for the alert and well-informed race goer. By carefully analysing the merit of each horse in a race and by assessing their individual racing characteristics it is possible to locate the two or three principals and perhaps the winner in any given race.

Q3 How does a horse go about getting a handicap mark?

The majority of horses begin their racing careers in two-year-old maiden races, some, a smaller number, in three year old maiden races, all carrying the same weight. After three runs they are given a rating, sooner if they win. The higher the rating achieved the better the horse. Thereafter they compete in two-year-old nursery handicaps. Their form rating, or handicap mark, will be reviewed, up or down, each time they run; each time, every time throughout their racing career until they retire at 5 or 6 years.

Two-year-old horses compete only against their own age group. Three-year-olds have their own races but can also race against older horses. And when they do, because they are not fully mature, they receive a weight allowance, which decreases throughout the season of their three-year-old career. As stamina also develops with maturity this weight allowance is not uniform and differs with the distance the younger horses have to run.

You can expect a horse to steadily improve up to maturity at about 5 years and their rating should reflect this. However the rate and extent of the improvement varies from horse to horse and can be difficult to predict. Some horses, the talented ones with Group potential, usually have more improvement in them than the others. Some horses improve slowly, some quickly and dramatically and some hardly at all. The well-bred horses with classic potential tend to be brought on much more slowly and deliberately than the majority. This is to ensure that they learn their job properly and thoroughly and are not harmed, physically or mentally, by being asked to do things in training or on the racetrack that they are not prepared for. Some older horses can surprise by making unexpected and significant improvement usually due to a change of scenery or a new regime under a different trainer. So predicting the amount and rate of natural improvement in a horse is a skill the race goer needs as it plays an important part in any selection routine.

This is particularly so when 3 year olds are racing against older horses. The younger horses receive a weight for age allowance, which decreases over the flat season, March to November, as they mature. As the 3 year olds lose their weight allowance they should be improving with maturity and so make up for the loss of the weight advantage by increased performance arising from being physically more developed. However being flesh and blood creatures their progress is never uniform. Some will mature and improve slowly, others more quickly. And the progress they make, at whatever rate, will generally not be consistent but coming in spurts. That is the challenge you face in your selection process. Each animal is different so you must decide on a case-by-case basis how much and at what rate each horse is improving. Probably the best way to discover the scale of improvement in any horse is to consult the private handicap, particularly **_Timeform._** Please refer to the example on the next page, featuring Ollie George.

On the right hand side by each horse's entry are the form figures for the last 6 runs with the most recent at the top of the column. From this you can tell whether there is a pattern of regression or improvement, or if the performance is not consistent, what type of ground or track may have caused the inconsistency. Or indeed some problem the horse may have had. It is an invaluable piece of information.

Timeform last 6 runs ratings summary
(On the right-hand side below the master form rating of 108)

7	**OLLIE GEORGE (IRE)**	5 8-12		**108**

7   **OLLIE GEORGE (IRE)**   5 8-12   **108**

ch.g. Fruits of Love (USA) 127 – The Iron Lady (IRE) (Polish Patriot (USA) 128) [2007 11.7f* 14.1m² 14g⁵ :: 2008 11.7d³ 12m⁴ 12m³ Jun 15] good-topped gelding: fairly useful handicapper: won at Bath in 2007: off 11 months (reportedly due to an injury), as good as ever this year, in frame all 3 starts, travelling well in touch to over 2f out when 2½ lengths third of 11 to Paktolos at Salisbury on latest: stays 1¾m: acts on polytrack, firm and good to soft going: effective visored or not: reliable. (110'Sb14m 103Nm12m 96'Nm14g)

		84
12m	108	84
12m	105	85
12d	108	85
14g'	109	87
14m'	110	87
12f'	106	+80

A. M. BALDING   L. P. Keniry Drawn 2

Royal blue, pink epaulets, white sleeves, royal blue and pink quartered cap (Mr Peter R. Grubb)

*In this example of Ollie George you can see that in his last six runs he has been fairly consistent; running to a maximum form rating of 110 and a minimum of 105. It tells us that he has probably plateaued and it also tells us that his best performances were both over 14 furlongs. The best recent performance was 5 races ago when, according to **Timeform**, he ran to a form rating of 110 over 14 furlongs on good to firm ground at Salisbury when his handicap mark was 87. In that race, where he came second, he also achieved his best speedfigure of 110.*

In this race, which is also 14 furlongs, he is on an official mark of 84, 3lb less than his very good run at Salisbury. He looks to be in good form and well handicapped, particularly over 14 furlongs.

Races to best avoid. I have concentrated in this book on Group races and Handicaps, as these comprise the majority of races in the UK. They are fathomable and can be worked out by logic and elimination. There are other races; Sellers and Claimers, and I have deliberately not covered these as they are best avoided because they involve lowly rated or un-trustworthy animals and the outcome can be very difficult to predict. Also in claimers the weight carried is determined, not by the horse's ability, but by the price the horse can be claimed for at the end of the race. I also find that Nursery handicaps can be difficult to predict as two year olds are still learning their craft and some can make rapid headway and some can even, temporarily, regress. I find this to be true of three-year-old handicaps too. Often in three-year-old handicaps many of the runners are trying a distance for the first time, some are improving rapidly, some slowly and the general upshot is a race that is difficult to fathom. But don't let me put you off these because I know other people find them a source of fun and a great betting medium.

Q4 How does the handicapping system work in practice?

Let's examine a handicap race in a little more detail to see how the rating and handicap system works in practice: The example is **The Royal Bank of Scotland Handicap,** (Class 4), at Ayr

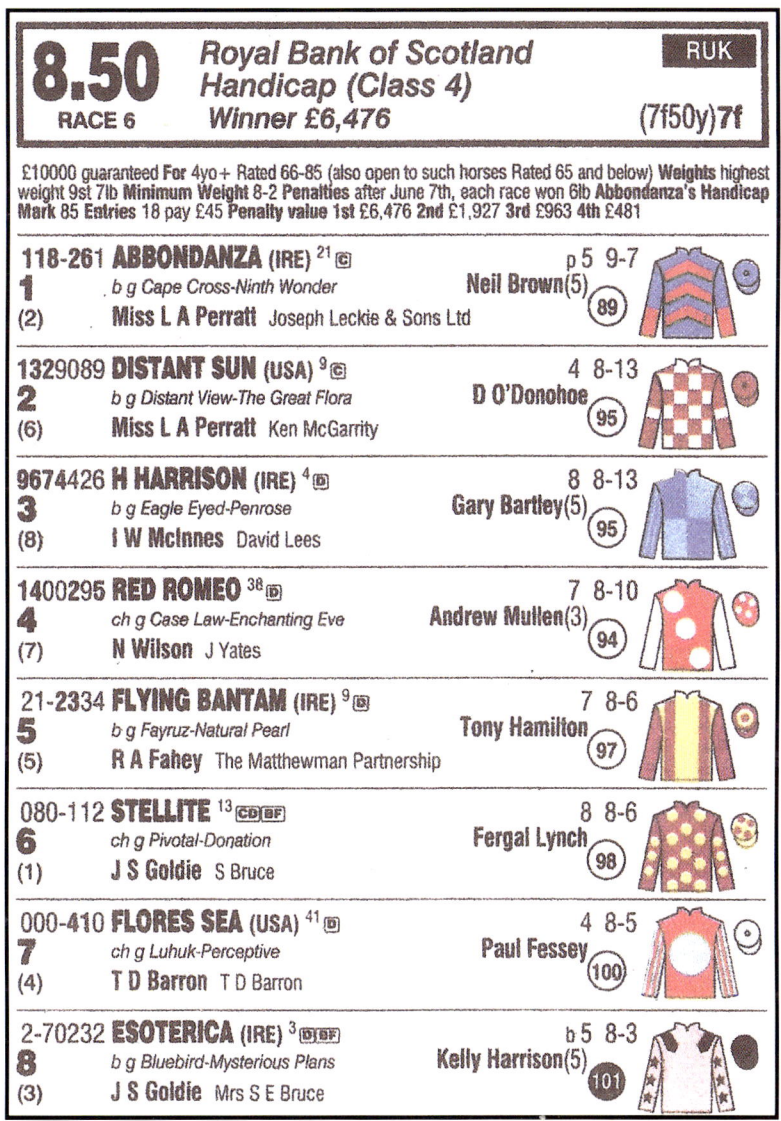

If you read the race conditions at the top of the race card you will see that this race is for horses aged 4 years plus, rated 66 to 85 and that the top weight allotted for this race is 9st.7lb. **Abbondanza** is the highest rated horse in the race with a handicap mark of 85; it therefore carries the top weight of 9st.7lb as dictated by the conditions of the race. **Distant Sun** and **H Harrison** both carry 8lb less than **Abbondanza** so they must both be rated 77. **Red Romeo** is carrying 3lb less than **Distant Sun** and **H Harrison** and must be rated 74…and so on down the handicap. **Esoterica** is carrying the bottom weight of 8st 3lb, which is 18lb less than **Abbondanza**; **Esoterica** must therefore be rated 67, 1lb above the official minimum prescribed at 8st.2lb.

The race conditions state that the race is for horses rated 66-85 but horses rated 65 and below can enter so long as the number of runners allows and that they meet the minimum weight requirements. To allow horses rated 65 or less meet the minimum weight requirements the top weight would be raised by a few lb. The absolute maximum weight for a flat race is 10st.0lb and the absolute minimum is 7st.12lb

In theory, if the handicapper has done a good job, these horses should finish quite close to each other. You will hear, on the box, experts opining that horse **X** is18lb better than horse **Y**. In this example **Abbondanza**, according to the handicapper, is 18lb better than **Esoterica**, which means that in this race **Abondanza** should finish 18 lengths in front of **Esoterica** *without the benefit of the handicap*. However with the effect of the handicap weighting they should, in theory, finish together.

The BHA's handicapper will review each horse's form rating after they have run. The handicapper will also often use other horses as yardsticks to asses the performance of a particular runner when re-rating it. If a horse has won or been placed it is likely that its rating will go up and it will be raised a few lb in the handicap, making it a little more difficult for it to win again. On the other hand, if a horse loses it is likely to be dropped a few lb. Horses tend to be raised in larger increments by the handicapper when they win and dropped much more slowly when they lose. The whole process is very dynamic and always under review.

In Group races the best horse in the race usually wins because they are all competing on ability on more or less equal terms. In handicaps the best 'weighted' horse, or the horse most leniently treated by the handicapper usually wins. Of course the normal caveats, regarding pace and going conditions, apply to these statements.

So to summarise: establishing the merit of a horse is done officially by the BHA and is encapsulated in a number; the BHA rating (alias form rating or handicap mark). Because the BHA handicapper reviews every horse's performance each time it runs the rating is always current and can tell you approximately the quality of a horse and whether it is improving or regressing. We have covered the main types of contests: handicap and group races that are both banded to ensure those of similar ability compete against each other. We have also looked at the mechanics of Handicap and Group races to see how they operate in practice. In Group races the horses compete equally against each other on merit; in Handicaps horses are weighted in order to equalise each horse's chance of winning.

*Consider the following **form summaries** or **race records** from the **Racing Post**; we can learn an awful lot about a horse and its preferences from these:*

Wigwam Willie: 6 year old bay gelding

Wigwam Willie				10-0
6-y-o b g Indian Rocket - Sweet Nature (Classic Secret)				
K A Ryan				Paul Mulrennan

Placings: 6104/0104010-4300313					Draw: 11
OR84		Starts	1st	2nd 3rd	Win & Pl
All Flat races		31	5	3 3	£43,132
80	6/08	Ripn	1m2f Cls4 65-83 Hcap good	......£4,857	
80	9/07	Ayr	1m Cls4 75-85 Hcap soft	............£6,477	
80	6/07	Newc	1m Cls4 64-82 Hcap heavy	........£6,232	
77	9/06	Ayr	1m Cls4 74-85 Hcap gd-sft	.........£6,477	
79	10/05	Donc	7f Cls4 70-84 App 3yo Hcap heavy £7,085		
			Total win prize-money £31,128		
GF-HRD 0-0-4		GS-HVY 4-3-13	Course 1-1-2	Dist 1-0-2	

Runs: Wigwam Willie has had 31 races; 5 wins, 3 second places and 3 thirds, the rest unplaced.

Rating: his current BHA, or official rating is 84. His first win was in November 2005 as a three year old, he was rated 79. Since then he has won races rated 77, 80, 80, and 80. All his wins have been achieved within a 3lb band; 77 to 80. As he is now 6 years old and has probably plateaued, it is unlikely he can win off his current mark of 84, unless he has a good claimer on board.

Track: it appears he has no preference regarding course orientation having won on both left handed and right-handed tracks.

Distance: as he has got older the distances he has won at have gone up from 7f to 8f (3 times) to 10f (latest).

Going: It appears he favours ground with plenty of give; his wins being achieved on good, good to soft, soft, and heavy going (twice). That's when, it appears, he's at his best.

Generous Jem: 5 year old bay mare

Generous Jem				10-0
5-y-o b m Generous - Top Jem (Damister)				
G G Margarson				Adrian McCarthy

Placings: 04/327311126-79					Draw: 1
OR81		Starts	1st	2nd 3rd	Win & Pl
Turf		12	3	2 1	£20,258
All Flat races		13	3	2 2	£20,739
74	9/07	Thsk	1m4f Cls4 72-79 Hcap gd-fm	......£6,477	
68	9/07	York	1m6f Cls4 62-73 Hcap gd-fm	......£6,477	
59	8/07	Newb	1m4f Cls5 50-69 Hcap good	.......£3,239	
			Total win prize-money £16,193		
GF-HRD 2-3-7		GS-HVY 0-0-3	Course 0-1-2	Dist 0-0-0	

Runs: Generous Jem has had 12 races on turf and 1 on the all weather; 3 wins, 2 second places and 1 third, the rest unplaced. We don't know whether she ran as a two and three year old or was just unsuccessful; being lightly raced one would suspect the former.

Rating: her current BHA rating is 81. All her wins came when she was a 4 year old. The first win was August 07 rated 59, the second September 07 rated 68 and the third also in September 07 rated 74. There may be some improvement to come but it looks unlikely as she has already run twice (so

far) in 2008, at Newmarket, without success and she is still on a mark 7lb higher than her last win. Probably 'in the handicapper's grip' for the moment.
Track*: All her wins have been achieved on left handed tracks, so she may be displaying a preference here.*
Distance*: Two of her wins have been at 12f and the other at 14f*
Going*:* *She has won twice on good to firm ground and once on good. She probably doesn't like too much cut in the ground.*

Hints and tips

The Race Record: can a horse win off its current rating?
• Before making a selection in a particular race it is useful to decide if the horses you are interested in are improving, have plateaued or are regressing.
• When you have made up your mind about their status then the Racing Record can be of great help to you in making a final selection.
• If one of the animals on your short list is currently on a higher form rating than all its previous wins but is still improving, it is possible that it could overcome the extra weight burden and go on and win again. If another has plateaued it is unlikely to succeed if its current mark is higher than all its previous wins. And, of course, if one is regressing it needs to be on a significantly lower rating to make an impression.

Hints and Tips

The Race Record: what ground does a horse prefer?
• The race record will also tell you on what ground/going a particular horse has won and most probably which ground it prefers.
• Some horses are very versatile and can win on almost any ground from hard to heavy.
• Others seem to win only within a narrow range of conditions for example, from good to good to firm.
• Some show a very distinct preference for a certain type of ground such as heavy and it is these animals that can be of interest, particularly if they perform on extremes of going which most other horses dislike.

How can this information about form and ratings help me in my selection?

When I say, in the preceding paragraph, that the BHA rating can approximately tell you the merit of a horse, I chose my words carefully because the official rating is only **one** person's opinion based on the evidence they've seen and is therefore subject to the whole panoply of weaknesses inherent in a largely qualitative judgement. Also giving an exact rating is difficult because of the nature of what you are trying to measure: i.e. racehorses, which are similar but not identical. They come in all shapes and sizes with a wide variety of physiques and temperaments, subject to differing training regimes, prone to injury and illness which can affect mood and confidence and in turn performance. Some also mature faster than others; they do not make uniform progress. Horses therefore, you would agree, cannot be accurately or exactly measured but do lend themselves to being expertly graded by comparative methods. In truth a large majority of the official ratings will be fairly accurate, some will be a little off the mark (plus or minus) and a further, probably smaller batch, will be way off.

Horses that were out of the frame in a race will probably miss the handicapper's scrutiny. One or two horses in a certain races could have been very unlucky in running and could well be several lb better than their current rating suggests. It is these mis-rated or under-rated horses that give you lots of opportunity, because the task of picking winners becomes a wee bit easier if you can ignore all those horses that you think are over-rated and concentrate on finding those in a race that are better than their official form rating suggests. So,

Do these under-rated animals really exist?

And if they do,

How do you locate them?

Q1 Do these under-rated animals exist?

I've suggested earlier that awarding a horse a rating is as much art as science because there is a degree of subjectivity involved, it is not an exact discipline. After a race has been run the handicapper has to weigh and assess the evidence and make a number of value judgements in order to re-rate the horses concerned based upon what he's seen and backed by his experience and expertise. No doubt there will be some anomalies to sort out and some contradictory data to reconcile before revised form ratings are allocated. At the end of the day it is the race as seen through the handicapper's eyes and his interpretation of the known evidence that determines the resultant rating. The handicapper will re-assess the winner and perhaps the placed horses in any race and could raise them anywhere from a couple of lb to several. The process is largely impressionistic and subjective and not 100% exact or perfect.

In addition to the horses leniently assessed by the handicapper you can definitely note down some of the unlucky runners in a race that did not make the frame. Unplaced horses do not normally get raised although some of them may have very valid excuses for not getting in the first three. They could have been unlucky in running; it could have been a falsely run race, they were given an un-enterprising ride or had a really bad draw. The excuses are endless. Some of these horses will end up with a rating that does not reflect their real ability. Therefore there are under-rated horses to be found (though not as many as over-rated) and this is an opportunity if you can locate them.

Q2 How do we find them?

The handicapper does not deal in 'what-ifs' but the punter can and should. It is usually the alert and well-informed race goer who succeeds in locating the under-rated horses based on acute observation, solid research and careful extrapolation.

When you go racing it is useful to learn to watch all the runners and riders in a race, and not just your selection. And let me stress that observing the jockeys can be just as productive as watching the horses. This way you can begin to spot potential and future winners. Race reading is a useful skill that you can build and develop with practice, patience, and experience. What should you be looking for?

Races are highly competitive events especially when there's a lot of prize-money or prestige at stake so always be on the lookout for 'incidents' or 'situations' that may occur in a race. Some horses may not have a trouble free journey and if you were aware of some incident they encountered during the race it can make their final finishing position look much better than it actually was. For example in the two-and-a-half minutes or so it takes to run a 12-furlong race an awful lot can happen. A horse can get blocked, checked, bumped, squeezed, hemmed-in, leant-on, have a bad start or a poor draw. Jockeys are always looking to find a good position in the field; the best ground, the shortest route and in the process they get impeded and impede others. Most of these incidents are accidental but some aren't, as jockeys will try to gain an advantage for themselves and attempt to put others at a disadvantage, all quite legally of course. These incidents or situations are worth observing and noting for they can affect the result and also help you highlight the unlucky runners.

The question is: 'What effect did one or more of these 'incidents' have on the unlucky horse and jockey'? Was the horse travelling well throughout the race, on the bit, despite its misfortunes? Did the said horse finish strongly from a poor position? And the jockey, how did he react? Was he 'rowing,' furiously throwing the reins at the horse to encourage it to no avail, or was he sitting confidently still knowing the horse had a lot more left to give? These signs will tell you either that the horse involved in the 'incident' would have lost anyway or whether it was truly unlucky and would have put up a very bold showing had it not been for the 'incident' or 'incidents' that you observed. If it was truly unlucky you may have found yourself an under-rated horse and a future winner. A final tip: always try to read up on the horses beforehand, if possible, to get to know their peculiarities and how they ought to be ridden to best effect so then you'll be able to recognise when they've been given a poor or un-enterprising ride.

Clearly it is impossible to describe all the different situations that can occur. Race reading is a skill that is very well worth developing. It needs time and patience in order to spot the important situations and incidents in a race and put the correct interpretation on them. Race reading will help you highlight the good and the under-rated horses. You'll find it a worthwhile investment of your time and energy.

Remember to follow up on the horses that go into your notebook. Check what the handicapper did with them subsequently. If they have been left on the same mark or have been reduced then you have probably got yourself an edge. The next time they run don't forget to check that the distance and the ground conditions will suit or you could be wasting your money.

Rounding The Bend
Roy Miller

A lot can happen in a race and it pays to watch all the runners in order to spot those that were really unlucky in running and have a genuine excuse. They will most likely, not be penalised and will have a weight advantage for their next race. Race reading is a skill worth developing.

If you don't have time, or are not yet confident enough to 'read' the races, then don't worry. There is another way of finding horses that are better than their official form rating. There are a number of **private handicaps** in existence. Organisations like *Timeform* and *Raceform* have their own team of handicappers and run a parallel form rating system to the BHA's. For example, the owner or trainer of a horse that runs well but finishes mid-division, because it met traffic problems, would be very unhappy to find that the official handicapper had raised it by 5lb or 7lb. The private handicaps are not so constrained and can reflect these good performances in their rating and also add a little commentary by way of corroborative detail. Their ratings are usually presented as overlays to the official handicap so you can compare, at a glance, the official rating with the private. The bigger the difference between the private and the official rating the better the chance that particular horse has. These private handicaps may cost a couple more pounds than the race card but they are well worth the investment. Here is an example from *Timeform*:

Timeform Private Handicap
8:30pm race at Goodwood, 14 furlongs, good to firm, June 2008
(See appendix for the *Timeform* guide to using the handicap and for abbreviations used)

FIFTH RACE GOODWOOD

8.30 RENAULT MASTER VANS STAKES (HANDICAP) (2) 1¾m

£20,000   4yo+   (Rated 0-100)   TWFA 4 9-13

---

1   TUSCULUM (IRE)   5 9-9   **108**

b.g. Sadler's Wells (USA) 132 – Turbaine (USA) (Trempolino (USA) 135) [2007 12v 15.5g Apr 9 :: 2008 NR] leggy, close-coupled gelding: smart performer in 2006, won listed race at the Curragh when also good 4¾ lengths fifth to Sixties Icon in St Leger at York (left with lot to do): left A. O'Brien 440,000 gns, useful form at best in 2 listed races (visored/in cheekpieces) in 2007 for A. Fabre, France: stays 1¾m: acts on soft and good to firm going: has hung, and is rather awkward.

95
15g' 108 L
12v' 97 L

A. P. STRINGER   Shane Kelly Drawn 7
Black, white hooped sleeves, red and white hooped cap (Curley Leisure)

---

2   BANDAMA (IRE)   5 9-5   **110**

b.h. Green Desert (USA) 127 – Orinoco (IRE) 53 (Darshaan 133) [2007 12m4 p10g2 12s 9.9g 12m 10m4 10m 12m3 12g2 12m :: 2008 12g2 Jun 7] big, lengthy, good sort: useful handicapper: placed at Kempton, Newmarket (not clear run) and Doncaster second/eighth/ninth starts in 2007: creditable head second of 15 to Bureaucrat at Epsom on reappearance, weaving through to be nearest finish: effective at 1¼m/1½m, should stay 1¾m: acts on polytrack, good to firm and good to soft going (tailed off both starts on soft): visored (failed to impress with finishing effort) seventh 4-y-o start. (109'Nm12m 97'Do12m 97'Nb10m)

91
12g 108 + 88
12m' 94   90
12g' 105   90
12m' 110 + 89
10m' 103   91
10m' 107   91

MRS A. J. PERRETT   Jim Crowley Drawn 5
White, red cross belts and armlets, yellow cap (Mrs S. L. Whitehead)

---

3   FORMAX (FR)   6 9-4   **107**

gr.g. Marathon (USA) 116 – Fortuna (FR) (Kaldoun (FR) 122) [2007 7.5d* 7.5g4 10.6d2 9.9g 7d 9m2 8m :: 2008 8s 9.9d2 8g5 12d* May 31] lightly-made gelding: useful performer: won 5 times in France, including handicap at Cagnes-sur-Mer in 2007: left J-C. Rouget after third 5-y-o start: easily best efforts in handicaps in Britain at Goodwood, squeezing through to lead well inside final 1f when winning 11-runner event on latest start by ¾ length from Akarem: stays 1½m: acts on soft and good to firm going. (92'Nm8m 87'Go10d 87'Go9m)

90
12d 106 + 85
8g   98 + 85
10d 107 + 83
8s   86
8m' 92   87
9m' 107   85

M. P. TREGONING   Pat Dobbs Drawn 8
Mauve, mauve and white check sleeves, white cap (Mr and Mrs A. E. Pakenham)

---

4   SWAN QUEEN   5 9-2   **111**

br.m. In The Wings 128 – Bronzewing 103 (Beldale Flutter (USA) 130) [2007 12d2 12g3 14d* 14s2 14g :: 2008 14.1g3 16g May 22] lengthy, angular mare: useful handicapper: improved further in 2007, winning at Sandown: shaped well when third of 9 to Wing Express at Salisbury on reappearance, unable to quicken having led on bridle 3f out: tailed off in Betty Barclay-Rennen at Baden-Baden last time: stays 1¾m: acts on soft and good to firm going: looked none too keen final 4-y-o outing. (87'Go14g 80Sb14g 77'Sa14d)

88
16g   93
14g 106 + 92
14g' 107   93
14s' 111 + 91
14d' 110 + 84
12g' 105 + 84

J. L. DUNLOP   Eddie Ahern Drawn 4
Red, green cap and striped sleeves (Sir Thomas Pilkington)

32

5 LEPIDO (ITY) 4 9-0 **107**

86

b.g. Montjeu (IRE) 137 – Luv Is For Sharing (USA) (Miswaki (USA) 124) [2007 10m^6 :: 2008 12m 10.3m^4 May 31] useful-looking gelding: fairly useful performer: won maiden and minor event at Milan in 2006 for B. Grizzetti: respectable last of 6 to Salford Mill in listed event at Newmarket sole 3-y-o outing: suffered stress fracture of tibia after, then gelded: respectable fourth of 7 to Ezdiyaad in handicap at Doncaster last time: should stay 1¼m: raced very freely on reappearance. (98'Nm10m 76Do10m 49Yo12m)

10m	98	90
12m	69	93
10m'	102	L

L. M. CUMANI   Seb Sanders Drawn 3
Dark blue, white chevron, red sleeves and cap (Mr P. Makin)

6 SHELA HOUSE 4 8-13 **111**

85

ch.g. Selkirk (USA) 129 – Villa Carlotta 110 (Rainbow Quest (USA) 134) [2007 8d^6 7m^2 8.1d^3 8.3d^3 10d* 10d^3 :: 2008 p10g^5 11.6g^3 12m^3 May 23] lengthy gelding: has a round action: fairly useful handicapper: won at Windsor in 2007: back to form last 2 starts, no chance with first 2 when 7¼ lengths third of 10 to Punjabi at Newmarket on latest, patiently ridden and staying on well final 2f: stays 1½m: acts on polytrack, good to soft and good to firm ground. (108Nm12m 99Wi12g 92'Wi10d)

12m	111	+85
12g	108	84
p10g	99	+84
10d'	106	+82
10d'	105	+76
8d'	91	+M

J. R. FANSHAWE   Richard Hughes Drawn 1
Bottle green, white cap, lime green star (Mr J. H. Richmond-Watson)

7 OLLIE GEORGE (IRE) 5 8-12 **108**

84

ch.g. Fruits of Love (USA) 127 – The Iron Lady (IRE) (Polish Patriot (USA) 128) [2007 11.7f* 14.1m^2 14g^5 :: 2008 11.7d^3 12m^4 12m^3 Jun 15] good-topped gelding: fairly useful handicapper: won at Bath in 2007: off 11 months (reportedly due to an injury), as good as ever this year, in frame all 3 starts, travelling well in touch to over 2f out when 2½ lengths third of 11 to Paktolos at Salisbury on latest: stays 1¾m: acts on polytrack, firm and good to soft going: effective visored or not: reliable. (110'Sb14m 103Nm12m 96'Nm14g)

12m	108	84
12m	105	85
12d	108	85
14g'	109	87
14m'	110	87
12f	106	+80

A. M. BALDING   L. P. Keniry Drawn 2
Royal blue, pink epaulets, white sleeves, royal blue and pink quartered cap (Mr Peter R. Grubb)

8 FREGATE ISLAND (IRE) 5 8-6 **108**

78

b.g. Daylami (IRE) 138 – Briery (IRE) 66 (Salse (USA) 128) [2007 10.9m^3 11m* 14g 12g^2 p12g^5 p12.2g :: 2008 p10g p10g^2 p11g^2 p12g* 11.6g^2 16g^4 May 30] tall, angular gelding: fairly useful performer: in good form of late, winning claimer at Kempton (claimed from J. Given £16,000) in February by 1¾ lengths from Given A Choice: 4¾ lengths fourth of 5 to Numero Due in handicap at Musselburgh last time: stays 2m: acts on polytrack and good to firm going: races prominently. (101Ms16g 101'Wa11m 99Wi12g)

16g	106	78
12g	108	75
p12g	108	C
p11g	108	75
p10g	106	C
p10g	97	80

A. G. NEWCOMBE   Fergus Sweeney Drawn 6
Orange, dark green disc (Mr Paul Moulton)

The top rated horses from the private handicap in the 8:30 race at Goodwood are:

Shela House 111
Swan Queen 111
Bandama 110

On closer inspection of the form summary, covering the last 6 runs, it shows that **Shela House** *has not run further than 12 furlongs and his best speed figures are over 12 furlongs too.* **Swan Queen** *has run over 14 furlongs four times in the last 6 runs. The best of these was on soft ground four races ago when she earned a* **Timeform** *rating of 111+. Her best speed figure of 87 was achieved at Goodwood on good going.* **Bandama** *has not run further than 12 furlong and his best speed figures are over 12 furlongs. From this group only* **Swan Queen** *is worth a second look, the other 2 can be dropped from the reckoning.*

The next best-rated are:

Ollie George 108
Fregate Island 108
Tusculum 108

Ollie George *has run over 14 furlongs twice in his last 6 runs, the best being 5 races ago when he achieved a form rating of 110 on good to firm ground! His best speed figure of 110 was also over 14 furlongs on good to firm ground. Interesting!* **Fregate Island** *has not run over 14 furlongs for 10 races, that was on good to firm ground and he was unplaced. His best speed figure of 101 was achieved on good ground over 16 furlongs.* **Tusculum** *has been off the track for more than a year. However he has run over 15 furlongs on good ground. There are no speed figures available for him.*

From this group **Ollie George** *looks very interesting.*

Finally we have:

Formax 107
Lepido 107

Formax *has not run over 14 furlongs, his best rating of 107 was achieved over 10 furlongs on dead ground and his best speed figure of 82 was over 8 furlongs on good to firm ground.* **Lepido** *too has not run over 14 furlongs. His best rating was over 10 furlongs on good to firm ground and his best speed figure of 98 was over 10 furlongs on good to firm ground. None from this group are of interest*

Only two horses appear to have good form over 14 furlongs; **Swan Queen** *and* **Ollie George**. *They are interesting contenders. Let's compare them a little more closely.* **Swan Queen** *received a form rating of 110+ but that was on dead ground, this race is on good to firm.* **Ollie George's** *best form rating was 110 on good to firm ground so he is proven at the distance and on the going. This is reinforced by his speed figure of 110 on good to firm ground.* **Swan Queen's** *best speed figure of 87 was on good ground. By logical deduction and elimination using the data provided by the private handicap we arrive at the selection of* **Ollie George.**

You will not be surprised to learn that **Ollie George** *won this race at odds of 7-1.*

This example has a couple of strong messages:

1. *Do not pick the top rated horse without checking over what distance and what ground the horse earned its form rating.*
2. *The speed figure can also give a strong indication of the horse's favoured ground and distance as well as its merit. (And maybe type of track: Note* **Ollie George** *got his best form and speed rating over 14 furlongs on good to firm ground at Salisbury, a downland track similar to Goodwood)*

Notes: In a handicap, with the official weight differentials as per the race card, the horses should finish pretty much together. However according to **Timeform's** *private handicap* **Shela House** *and* **Swan Queen** *(111) are 1lb better than* **Bandama** *(110), 3lb better than* **Ollie George**, **Fregate Island** *and* **Tusculum** *(108), and 4lb better than* **Formax** *and* **Lepido** *(107). But you can see from the above analysis that it is always worth checking on what ground and at what distance these horses earned their* **Timeform** *Private Handicap Rating and making your own appropriate adjustments.*

Hints and tips

Using the private handicap
With horse racing it very often pays not to pick the bleeding obvious so:
• Don't necessarily go for the top rated horse:
○ It may not have gained its rating over this distance
○ It may not appreciate today's going
○ It may not like the track – so check each one out
• There may be in the line-up a rapid improver or a very dark horse worth a serious second look.
• There may be a horse that has been campaigned over the wrong distance recently but has respectable form over this trip.
• There may be a horse that saves its best performances for this course or this trip.
• If there are extremes of going, hard or heavy, look for the horse with good form on such going. There won't be many.
Check out all possibilities before making your decision, and you may find it isn't the top rated horse.

GoingStick readings

FROM December 2003, going descriptions for 15 top racecourses contain GoingStick readings on the following scale:

1-2.9	Heavy	5-6.9	Good to Soft	11-12.9	Firm
3-4.9	Soft	7-8.9	Good	13-15	Hard
		9-10.9	Good to Firm		

Chapter Three

Establishing the Merit of a Horse

Speed

**Lord Hippo suffered fearful loss
By putting money on a horse
Which he believed, if it were pressed
Would run faster than the rest.
Hilaire Belloc**

It's clear that poor old Lord Hippo had never heard of speedfigures.

In my opinion there are two ways of assessing the true merit or ability of a horse: the form rating and the speed or time figure. Officially only form counts in determining a horse's merit, that's what the handicapper uses in assessing each horse's performance relative to all the others. However speed always speaks for itself; it's the horse against the clock. If accurately measured there can be no doubting the merit of a speedfigure; the horse ran fast! Form can be very subjective, as it takes no account of how the race was run. Only the quality of the animals the winner beat is taken into consideration.

Experts can and do argue over the merit of a form figure. Exactly how good was the performance? Was the race truly run? What quality of animals did the winner beat? There should be no such arguments over a speedfigure. If a horse has posted a fast time, that's it…it's a fast time, no argument, no debate. For example if a horse wins a race and in the process beats some smart performers but in a slow time, was it a good performance? The answer is we just don't know. It could be. No doubt the horse will be given a better or improved form rating. If a horse wins a race, any race, in a fast time, was that a good performance? The answer is definitely, most definitely Yes, Oh! Yes! There is no gainsaying a good speedfigure.

However a good horse may not register a respectable speedfigure for a variety of reasons; it may have been running over the wrong distance, on unsuitable going, against mediocre opposition or god forbid, it might not be fully fit. Often the main reason is want of opportunity through lack of pace in its races to date. If horses run too fast or too slow early on in a race the final time will be adversely affected. If they run too slowly they can't make up the time in the later stages of the race, if they run too quickly then they will tire themselves out before the end. In either case the result is a mediocre speedfigure. A strong, sustainable pace is key to a horse achieving a good speedfigure, that and of course, ability. That's why in major races a pacemaker is often introduced into the line-up to ensure a truly run race to try to guarantee that the best horse will win.

To make them readily understandable or comprehensible most natural phenomena can be measured and expressed as a number; IQ's, blood pressure, temperature etc. And of course it is possible to express the time taken to run a horse race in a number or speedfigure for each animal participating. Calculating your own speedfigures is very, very time consuming, with about 9,000-

10,000 horses in training at any one time there's just too many to keep tabs on if you're not doing it full time. It's also a job that takes years to master, requiring a great deal of skill, judgement and experience. Therefore it's a much more efficient use of your time to use those figures compiled by the experts. However it is useful to understand the main ingredients that go into the equation used to calculate them in order to comprehend fully the dynamics of speed rating and to better judge which compiler produces the most accurate figures.

Throughout this chapter on speed, in order to illustrate the difficulty and complexity of establishing reliable speedfigures in the UK, I will compare and contrast British racing with that of the USA. It will also help us better understand not only the essentials and variables that go into the equation for calculating speedfigures but also why they are introduced.

In the USA race goers use speedfigures routinely when making their selection and **The Daily Raceform** makes a major feature of their **Beyer Speedfigures** not only for the races but also for their track training workouts. Why is this? Because most tracks in the USA are the same, completely uniform: oval, flat, dirt, left-handed and a mile round. In races in the US there is also only a few pounds difference in weight carried between the top and bottom rated horses. As a result the figures are relatively easy to calculate, it is a simple sum to convert the time taken to cover a given distance on a uniform surface with very few variables to consider and little or no adjustment for weight carried. Therefore a horse running six furlongs at Bay Meadows in San Francisco should post roughly the same time as a horse of similar merit running six furlongs at Aqueduct in New York; any difference pointing to the ability of the horse concerned. You can compare the time performances with little or no adjustment. Contrast and compare this with the UK.

Here it's not so easy because racing in the UK throws up far more variables:

- **The tracks** are all different. None are even remotely alike
- A greater variety of **going conditions** are produced on turf
- There is normally a huge range in **weights** carried
- **Weather** conditions, **particularly wind** velocity and direction can change quickly or often during the course of a race meeting

The tracks are all different, the topography, configuration and conformation do vary enormously. Some are flat, some mainly uphill, some mainly downhill and some are undulating in nature. Some have a few big, gradual, sweeping bends and some have sharper ones. All these disparate physical characteristics of the UK courses affect the times taken to run the races. Unlike the USA tracks, you are never comparing apples with apples. For example, a horse running six furlongs at Pontefract which is mainly uphill will, on average, be more than 7 or 8 seconds slower than a horse running six furlongs at Epsom which is all downhill. York, which is flat, produces times that are about 5 seconds slower than Epsom for six furlongs. So due to individual track idiosyncrasies in configuration and conformation race times vary significantly from course to course.

Racing in the USA is mainly on dirt, which is either standard or sloppy with not much else in between. In the UK racing is mainly on turf which, due to the effect of sun, soil and rain, throws up many different **going conditions** from hard to heavy with a lot in between, all of which affect race times. Officially these going conditions range from hard, firm, good to firm, good, good to soft,

soft, and heavy. For example a six furlong listed race at Doncaster run on **good to firm** ground produced a time of **1min 12.30secs,** later in the same year another six furlong listed race run on **heavy ground** produced a time of **1min 19.08secs;** nearly seven seconds slower, which represents about a 10% fluctuation in race time! As you can see the track conditions have a material effect on the time clocked.

In the USA there is very little difference between top and bottom **weight** in a race, rarely more than seven pounds. In fact the American speed guru *Andrew Beyer* discounts weight from his calculations altogether. Even here some experts appear agnostic about the effect of weight on a horse's performance even though in a handicap race in the UK there can be a spread of two stone or more in a race. An average racehorse tips the scales at about 950lb plus, so a nine and a half stone jockey represents about 12% of the horse's weight. An average bloke weighs in at about 12 stone so if you put 16lb of spuds in a haversack on his back and told him to run four or five hundred yards as fast as he could he might give you an opinion about the effect of weight on performance. I think it is hard to ignore the effect of the weight carried on the final time of a race!

On a very blustery day with cold cross **winds** and head winds blowing over the tops at Beverly, whistling across the plains at Newmarket or howling over the sea at Yarmouth at 30 or 40 miles per hour and hitting a 950lb mass also travelling at 30 or 40 miles an hour in the opposite direction, then it's bound to slow them up a wee bit! Wind can indeed have a significant effect on race-times!

The challenge is to reconcile all the race variables; course, going, weight, wind and to give a single accurate time figure expressed as a number; a high number being fast and a low number being slow. Then we can compare the figures produced and tell which is the superior performance. For example is a time of 1min 12.3secs for 6F at Doncaster carrying 9st.2lb on good to firm ground better or worse than 1min 15.3secs for 6F at Windsor carrying 9st.8lb on soft going? Or is 2mins 53.5secs for 12F at Folkestone carrying 9st.0lb on soft ground better or worse than 2mins 33.2secs for 12F at Carlisle carrying 8st.7lb on firm ground? It is not at all immediately obvious is it?

So how do you determine how fast a horse has run and produce an accurate, reliable speedfigure? Given the above information you'd imagine it would be very difficult or near impossible to do, but believe it or not it is a bit easier than you may think. However experts vary in their approach to working out speed ratings, and you can tell because of the variable success rates between speed rating compilers. Their basic equations, used to calculate the figure, are more or less the same. They just place slightly different weightings on the elements that make up the equation. For example you may find that the standard or benchmark times they use may differ a little from each other and that the formulae used to calculate the going allowances may also vary a bit. So I have set out below the **general principles**, not the nuts and bolts, of how speedfigures for horses racing in the UK are usually calculated.

The first task is to bring all the various running times into line, to establish a set of benchmark or standard times for all racecourses in the UK. Any individual or organisation intent on producing speedfigures for all flat horses must have race records for all courses going back several years. By taking an average of the times recorded over the designated period and adjusting for weight carried above and below a norm of 9st.0lb it is possible to establish for each **course** a reliable set of standard times for all races advertised. So a horse achieving standard time carrying 9st.0lb on good ground can be speed rated 100. This allows for **weight** differentials to be adjusted, for example a horse carrying 8st.10lb, four pounds less than the norm, would be speed rated 96 and a horse carrying 9st.10lb would be speed rated 110.

The final task, and probably the most difficult, is to determine the effect of the going conditions on the time of the race. The going conditions, ground and wind, can help produce faster times on firm ground and slower times on soft ground and need to be taken account of in the final time figure. This is done by applying, a very aptly named, 'going allowance' to each race. Fractions of a second are either added to or subtracted from the time for each furlong in a race depending upon conditions. Hard ground allows horses to run faster by about minus 0.65 seconds per furlong against standard time and heavy ground can slow horses up by as much as plus 1.40 seconds per furlong against standard time. These figures may not appear significant but taken cumulatively they can have a marked effect on a race. For instance a going allowance of minus 0.20 second per furlong faster than standard time in a six-furlong sprint is worth 1.2 seconds for the race. When you consider that a sprinter can cover nearly 20 yards in this time and that equates to several lengths at the finish.

Setting the going allowance for a race requires great skill and experience. The compiler has to assess the ground, whether certain sections of the course have been watered or not, judge the quality of the horses participating, the wind direction and effect and how the race was run, (truly or falsely run) before setting it. That requires a very good knowledge of all flat tracks in the UK, a certain competence in race reading and vast experience of how ground and wind conditions are likely to affect the speed. This is another very good reason to leave the job to the experts.

So, in summary, speedfigures are calculated by taking the actual race time and:

a) Adding or subtracting the going allowance (per furlong)
b) Working out the difference compared to the course standard time (after calculating it, hopefully correctly)
c) Adjusting for weight carried

I suggested at the head of this chapter that you should eschew compiling your own speedfigures because of the time and effort involved and use those constructed by the experts. I also covered the essential elements that go into working out speedfigures as it may also assist you in assessing who produces the most accurate ratings and thus which to use.

Of course the late, great Phil Bull, who founded *Timeform* after the war, was a speedfigure pioneer. In fact in the 1930's under the nom de guerre *William Temple* he was selling his speedfigures to private clients with great success for all parties concerned. *Timeform* therefore have a great deal of experience in all aspects of speed rating and by now they should know what works and what doesn't when assessing speed and their figures appear pretty reliable. *Raceform* is another organisation that produces accurate figures and are also well worth considering. However to begin with it is worth checking out two or three in your selection routine and evaluating who you think is the more accurate. It's also worth remembering that while the pen name of the speed compiler in the racing comics stays the same the individual operating under it can change, and so can the quality of output, therefore always stay critical and alert.

How can speedfigures help you?

Speedfigures are a powerful tool in your selection armoury. A good speedfigure will mark out a horse of special or exceptional ability well before the form lines confirm it, thereby giving you an advantage over the less informed. One or two points difference in speed is not really big enough to pinpoint a selection given the vagaries of track or ground conditions. Several points difference should give you a little more confidence and if it's double digit you should really sit up and pay attention. Do not, repeat, do not follow the speedfigures blindly. Always check how the horse you are interested in made its speedfigure, what distance, what ground, what weight and also do not forget what jockey, before you make a final selection. Speedfigures can also help you find value in a race and where the horses all look much the same, can help in making that final decision on selection (See how we separated Swan Queen and Ollie George on page 34). Also when using speedfigures, from any publication, always make sure they have been adjusted for weight to be carried i.e. set to 9st.0lb and not given 'raw' or un-adjusted.

I'm always a little suspicious if a horse has a good form rating but a mediocre time figure. Agreed, this can be overlooked in lightly raced two or three year olds as they may not have had the opportunity to post a good time figure due to the lack of pace in their races to date. However it is hard to overlook a mediocre time figure in a well-campaigned three, four or five year old. When checking out the basic merit of a horse make sure their time figure is commensurate with the form figure. Or satisfy yourself that there is a sound reason for the discrepancy.

However if a lightly raced two or three year old has a good time figure and a mediocre form rating it is certainly worth noting. Because the time figure could be a good and early indication of its real merit long before the form lines become clear and frank its ability.

Check Up
Roy Miller

Some observations on betting strategies: Favourites and Value
• Only about 29% of favourites win. That's slightly less than 1 in 3! Not a great or encouraging ratio for the poor punter!
• Favourites therefore do not offer great value and are generally worth opposing
• I'm not saying don't back favourites, just be very, very sure when you do considering the risk/reward ratio
• Look for value. If you don't think there is value in the price offered shop around or leave alone.
• What is value? It really is your judgement. If you think as a result of your research into a race a certain horse ought to be short odds but you find it is 4 or 5 points longer, then that is probably good value. And vice-versa for poor value.

Some observations on betting strategies: Systems and Tipsters
• Betting systems are bookies friends. They are a way of losing money slowly and methodically. Usually they having nothing to do with the horse and its inherent ability but with peripheral, rather inconsequential data such as trainers, tracks, month of the year, certain types of races etc. Most bizarre! You'd probably be better off popping your money on the roulette wheel!
• Following tipsters does not help you learn about racing and forces you to participate almost vicariously.
• Your acquired knowledge of form, speed and race variables is better than any system ever devised and far superior to any tipster's naps, for you have formed the judgement yourself, added to your knowledge and expertise and probably had lots of enjoyment doing it.

Chapter Four

Racing Characteristics

Certain factors that can either aid or hinder a horse's performance

'Anyone wishing to make an ass of himself has only to issue an unqualified statement about a racehorse. The horse will take it from there.'
Humphrey Finney

In the introduction I said that the outcome of any horse race was determined by the relative merits of the horses participating and by the influence of a specific number of factors that can affect a horse's performance in either a positive or a negative way; the race variables. In chapters two and three I covered the principal ways of assessing a horse's basic ability: **form** - an assessment of merit based on how well they've run against other horses or what other horses they've beaten and **speed** - merit based on how fast they have run against the clock.

If you can understand what a horse is capable of, relative to others participating in a race, then you are more than halfway down the road to cracking the problem of who will win. All you have to do then is to check out the race conditions and match them against the horses' known predilections or preferences for going, distance, track etc., to ensure you get a tick in the box rather than a cross or a question mark. The horse with the most ticks (or least number of crosses) will most appreciate the prevailing race conditions. So in this chapter I'll cover the factors that can affect a horse's race performance and that need to be examined alongside form and speed when you are making your selection. These factors are:

Distance
Track
Going
Pace
Fitness and Health
The Jockey
Weight

Distance

Will the horse you are interested in get the trip?

When in his prime you'd probably have felt very confident about sticking a few quid on Linford Christie to win running over 100 or 200 meters. You might have thought twice about wagering on him if he were running over a mile. It's the same with horses, they are specialists and have a favoured distance, very often within no more than a couple of furlongs; 5 or 6 furlongs, 6 or 7 furlongs, 7 furlongs or a mile, 10 or 11 furlongs etc., etc.

There are 3 simple ways to check whether a horse will perform at the distance advertised.

History: The first is simple and obvious and that is to check their race record. Have they run at this distance before either winning or running with credit i.e. by posting a good time figure or running well against decent competition.

Breeding: If a horse has never run over a given distance before then it is as well to check their pedigree to see if there is a likelihood of them getting or appreciating the trip! The thoroughbred racehorse is a sublime mix of speed and stamina but the ratios of these two qualities vary according to how the horse was bred. Sprinters are nearly all-raw speed, stayers have bags of stamina and middle-distance performers have a balance. If the race record can't tell you if the horse will get the trip then where can you find some breeding information that might enlighten you? Every year ***Timeform*** publishes the *'Stallion Statistical Review'* that lists all the different stallions with progeny running in the UK. Contained within it is a table, which lists every stallion according to the average distance at which their offspring win (average winning distance or AWD). From this you can see which stallions produce sprinters, which produce middle distance runners and which produce stayers. It is not quite as simplistic as this but a good rule of thumb nevertheless. This information is of great practical value to the race goer for it gives a good indication whether a horse you are interested in is likely to be effective at the trip advertised. However these tables can only indicate the probable because the dam will also contribute her share of genes and will therefore affect the speed or stamina of the progeny.

Physique: The third way is to look at the physique for each type of horse: sprinters, stayers and middle-distance runners have slightly different physiques. If the breeding says they may get the trip it is worth double-checking with an appraisal of the physique to add a little more evidence. Sprinters are usually sturdy, barrel-chested animals, thick-necked with powerful quarters and a well-formed backside. Middle distance performers and stayers are usually lighter, leaner and carry less condition than sprinters.

The Track

There are three things here that can likely affect a horse's performance and they need careful examination before you make any selection:

1. The course orientation, is it left handed or right handed?
2. The topography or course conformation.
3. The effect of the draw.

Course orientation: Racecourses in the UK are either left-handed or right-handed; therefore there is a requirement for horses to be able to perform well on either orientation. Regrettably some show a decided preference for one or the other. It is always worth checking the form of a horse to see if it reserves its best performances for a particular type of track orientation to see if it shows a preference for running either clockwise or anticlockwise. You may discover that a really good horse, on the occasions that it has been beaten, may well be on a particular orientation.

Even group horses can be single threaded. Take Tudor Minstrel for example. He won the 2000 Guineas (a straight mile) by eight lengths, in a canter and was then installed as ante post favourite for the Epsom Derby. His meticulous trainer, Fred Darling, had constructed a replica gallop of the Derby course at his racing establishment at Beckhampton. Gordon Richards, the then champion jockey, rode him on his last piece of work there before the Derby but received a terrible, terrible shock! It was obvious to him that the horse's action was wrong and that he couldn't handle a left hand course at all. Which meant that poor old Tudor Minstrel would not handle Epsom, which is a very difficult course anyway and left handed to boot. The champion jockey confided that he had no idea how to ride him in the classic and neither did the champion trainer.

Tudor Minstrel took his chance in the Derby and Richards had a nightmare ride. Every time he held the horse up it fought him and every time he let it down it shot off to the right. Considering he couldn't handle a left-handed track he finished a creditable fourth. On raw ability he was probably the best horse in the race he just couldn't cope with the left handed track.

Course conformation and topography: Racecourses come in all shapes and sizes: flat, undulating, uphill, downhill, horseshoe-shaped, oval, triangular, some with sharp bends others with wide sweeping bends, some with short straights and others with long straights etc. Horses are versatile creatures and can handle most courses but there are some tracks that pose more than their fair share of problems. On these courses many horses either perform badly or throw in a less than average performance. However some horses seem unconcerned by the course peculiarities and perform well or very well. That is where the saying 'horses for courses' probably originates. Even jockeys are challenged by some of these courses; for example Kieren Fallon, several times champion jockey, is on record as saying he finds riding at Goodwood particularly difficult and demanding.

If your selection can cope with the oddities or peculiarities of some of these 'special requirement' courses then you will have an advantage. Courses such as Epsom, Brighton, Goodwood, Chester, Catterick and Pontefract put special demands on a horse and it is the horses with the special racing characteristics required that generally do well here. These course specialists seem to reserve their winning for such tracks where qualities such as nimbleness, extra stamina reserves, or good balance come in to play.

Prelude					9-8
7-y-o b m Danzero - Dancing Debut (Polar Falcon)					
W M Brisbourne			T G McLaughlin		
Placings: 65018123154-75623126				Draw: 10	
OR 72	Starts	1st	2nd	3rd	Win & Pl
Turf	40	5	7	5	£36,153
All Flat races	41	5	7	5	£36,153
66 7/08 Ches	1m4½f Cls5 49-66 Hcap gd-sft				...£4,094
66 8/07 Ches	1m4½f Cls4 65-84 Hcap gd-fm				...£5,505
58 7/07 Ches	1m4½f Cls5 58-75 Hcap heavy				...£3,617
52 6/07 Ches	1m4½f Cls5 51-70 Am Hcap good				£3,435
56 8/04 Ripn	1m2f Cls5 45-68 3yo Hcap gd-sft				£3,864
				Total win prize-money £20,515	
GF-HRD 1-2-13 GS-HVY 3-5-16 Course 4-4-14 Dist 4-5-19					

Prelude seems to reserve her winning performances for Chester

Galileo and Mick Kinane, Epsom Derby 2001
Roy Miller

Epsom racecourse has a number of idiosyncrasies; a steep downhill finish with a very odd camber, a steep rise from the middle distance starts, difficult bends... just to name a few of them

Effect of the draw: A 'good' draw can confer either one of two advantages. It can give access to better ground or, because there is no stagger, it can give a slightly shorter route to the winning post. Each course has its draw idiosyncrasies and it is worth getting to know them as sometimes they can have a bearing on the result. Here are a couple of examples:

Better ground: When you examine the straight 6 furlong sprint results at Ascot, (which should confer no draw advantage), you realise that a huge majority of the winners are drawn within 5 places from either the stand rail or the far rail thereby benefiting those drawn high or low. Why is this? This is because the watering system does not cover the track uniformly leaving the edges drier than the middle of the track. This makes the ground nearest both the rails much faster thus favouring those animals drawn there. The straight sprints at Ayr, Doncaster and Sandown Park, just to name a few, also seem to have a strong draw bias so it is worth getting to know what numbers are favoured and under what conditions the effect is pronounced.

Shortest route: At Goodwood on the 7-furlong course the draw favours those drawn high because of a long right-handed bend before the straight. As I've pointed out before, there is no stagger or allowance for the effect of the draw. So some horses have to run a little further than those with a favourable draw, or expend a lot more energy in the early stages of a race to try to get to the inside running rail. You can imagine at a tight circular course like Chester where they are nearly always running a bend, even in the sprints, that the effect of the draw can be quite pronounced.

It's impossible, in this modest volume, to list all the courses and all the races where there is a pronounced draw advantage and under what conditions they prevail. The message here is get to know your racecourses and which races confer draw advantages. Also under certain conditions the effects of the draw can be more pronounced and this can be really useful, advantageous information to the alert punter. You will find helpful notes regarding the effect of the draw in the **Racing Post** or at the front of the **Timeform** race card.

Going

I once had a share in a horse called *Astrac* who **Timeform** described as smart. Anyway, he was an above average performer but on soft or heavy going he was even better. When there was plenty of give in the ground, he was well and on a favourable handicap mark, we were always highly optimistic of a good run and were rarely disappointed. Don't get me wrong, because he was a good horse he did win on other sorts of going but his superlative performances were always on soft.

And I'm sure that all the evident performance improvement on soft wasn't down to him entirely; the other horses in the race probably couldn't handle the going as well as he did and they didn't run up to scratch thus making his performance look the more impressive. I don't think Astrac was unique by any means and no matter how good you think a horse is it could be a whole lot better (or worse) given certain ground conditions. So, before you confirm your choice, make sure that your selection will handle the ground and even better, may relish it. Remember the example of Wigwam Willie in chapter two; he did all his winning when there was plenty of cut in the ground, particularly when it was heavy.

Pace

The saying goes that **'the pace is the race'** or how a race is run has a significant impact on the result. The factors that can affect the pace of a race are:

1. The ability, alertness and enterprise of the jockey
2. The quality of the horses participating and their style of running
3. The riding instructions the jockeys receive

The ability and enterprise of the jockey: Being a dumb chum the poor old horse doesn't know how far it's got to run in a race and left to its own devices would gallop as fast as it could for as long as it could till it ran out of gas. Judging the pace of a race to suit the horse is the jockey's job! So it's very important to get to know those who are good at it and those who aren't.

In a race some jockeys just seem to accept the pace dictated to them without appearing to think about the consequences of a pace that's either too fast or too slow for their horse. If someone dawdles in front they'll dawdle along too or if some one goes hell for leather they'll probably follow suit. Then you'll get the jockeys who will try to be enterprising and make the pace only to get overhauled by several other horses in the straight because they couldn't judge the pace sufficiently well for their ride either making it too slow or too fast.

Don't get me wrong. The majority of jockeys are highly competent and professional but there is also a select band that seems to have a clock in their heads and who can judge the pace accurately and well. They instinctively know when the race is too fast or too slow for their mount and react appropriately. Lester Piggot and Steve Cauthen were the real maestros at judging the pace and there are some excellent judges of pace in today's line up of riding talent; Frankie Dettori, Seb Sanders, Michael Hills, Kieren Fallon to name but a few.

Such is the importance of getting the pace right for the horse that often superior horsemanship can win the race for an inferior horse. And the corollary is also true that poor jockeyship can get the best horse beaten. In any race you can say that the winning jockey got his riding plans right and the rest got theirs wrong, some spectacularly so. How about Dancing Brave when he came second to Sharastani in the 1986 Derby, by far and away the best horse in the race! In fact the best horse in Europe and probably the world at that time.

Sprint races usually pose no problems in the pace department for there is no time for hanging about and they are always truly run. However the further they run the more chance there is of a tactical or falsely run race developing. Which takes me on to my second point on pace:

The quality of the horses taking part and their favoured style of running: There is a saying in racing: 'The bigger the field the bigger the certainty!' Doesn't seem logical does it? However when you think about it, it does make sense. In a big field there is a greater likelihood of one, maybe two, horses cutting out a strong pace, going a really good gallop and causing the moderate horses to throw the towel in long before the finish and with the best horse usually going on to win after a tussle in the straight with those left. In a field with only a few runners there is likely to be a lot of messing about, cat and mouse stuff and they don't go a decent gallop until they hit the straight and in this case anything can win, even a moderate animal so long as they've got a bit of finishing speed. That is why in a small field, particularly in group races, owners or trainers with a fancied horse sometimes run a pacemaker to cut out a strong gallop thus ensuring the best horse wins. And for gawds sake make sure you do your homework and know which horse is the pacemaker so you don't back it! (Although they've been known to win very occasionally!)

Of course when judging the pace in a race the jockey has to take into consideration the horse's favoured style of running and adapt his tactics accordingly. The horse might like to be at the head of affairs, in the van, in the middle of the pack covered up or safely bringing up the rear and waited with. Here are a few excerpts from ***Timeform*** just to illustrate the point:

Impeller………………………'Usually waited with'
Road to Love…………………'Front runner'
Reefscap……………………'Ideally suited by being ridden prominently'
Tungsten Strike……………..'Usually races prominently'
Cover Up……………………'Usually patiently ridden'
Sergeant Cecil………………'Usually held up'

The owner's or trainer's instruction to the jockey: Then of course there are the instructions the jockey receives from the owner or the trainer, which will dictate how they ride the race. Trainers and their regular jockeys know their animals and how they prefer to run and their instructions are usually well aligned to the horse's favoured running style. But not always, for sometimes they may try something different as an experiment, particularly if the horse hasn't been running up to its known ability or sometimes just to surprise the rest of the field and catch them off guard. The instructions on how to run the race usually presuppose that the race won't be falsely run. If it is, the jockey should be empowered to take appropriate action to counteract it.

Generous
Roy Miller

The way he won the King George at Ascot was breathtaking

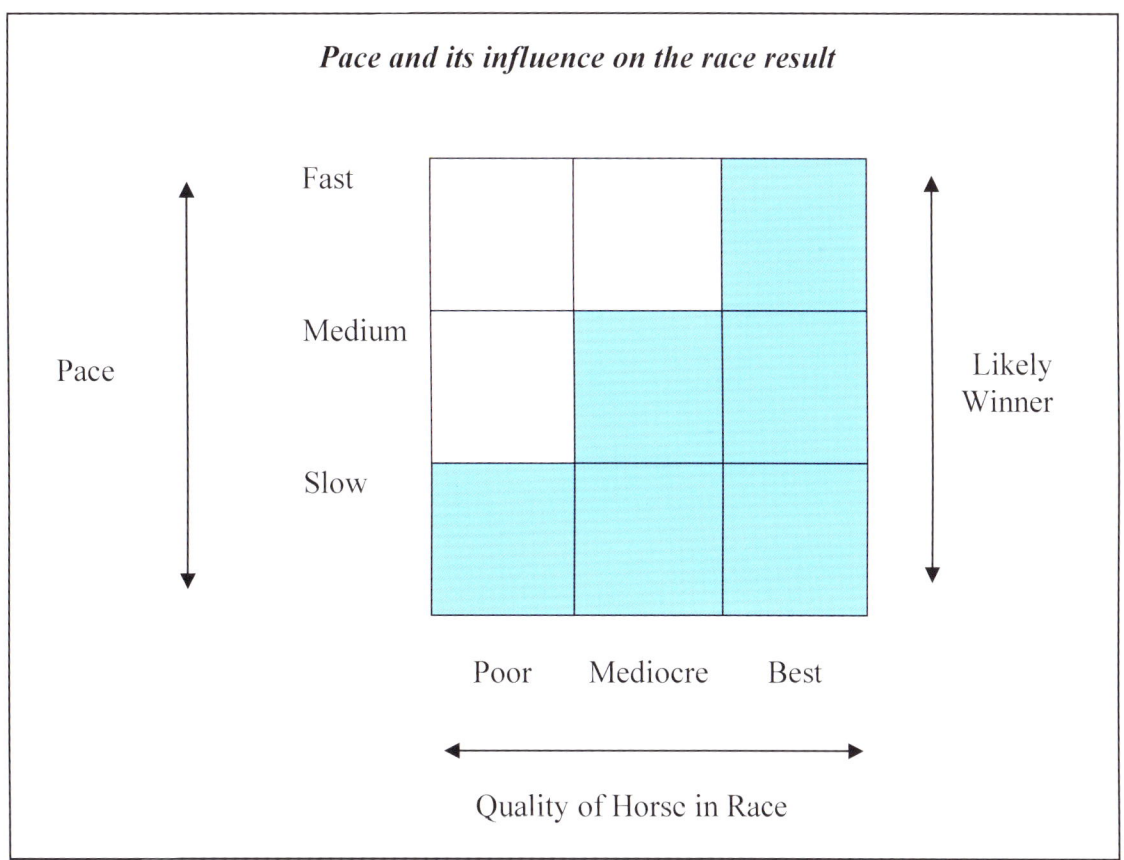

Pace and its influence on the race result

In summary the above chart is telling us that:

- If the pace if fast/optimised then the best horse in the line-up will win
- If the pace is average then either a mediocre or good horse could win
- If the pace is slow and tactical any horse in the line-up can win!

Fit and well

A trainer has a limited number of important jobs to do. To look after his owners, place his horses carefully and well and last but not least he has to get them fit and to keep them fit and well.

However, I would imagine that it is blindingly obvious that a horse will win its race only if it

1. **Has the ability**
2. **Is well**
3. **Is fit**

and the race variables (covered in this chapter) are in its favour. Seeking out the horse's ability is the easier bit and is done by desk research uncovering its form and time figures. Checking on its well-being and fitness is more difficult as you can only judge the two states from what you see of the animals on the racecourse or TV. You are not dealing with facts and data. You are forming an impression based on what you see. So you must learn to judge the signs of a healthy horse and a fit horse.

Health and well being: What are the signs that tell us a horse is healthy and that all other factors being equal it should run to its known potential? Clearly the best way to gauge a horse's health is to take its pulse, its temperature and maybe give it a blood test. However this isn't possible for the race goer; you can only judge on what you can see from an inspection of the animals in the paddock, pre-parade ring or going down to post. Luckily for us it is usually very evident from its appearance whether a horse is healthy or not from the condition of various parts of its body or anatomy.

So what are some of the outward signs of a healthy horse? The eyes should be big, bright and clear, the coat flat, smooth and glossy. No puffiness or swelling to the limbs. The general demeanour should be relaxed yet alert and interested.

To get and keep a horse healthy it needs a good, well balanced diet. It also needs exercise, good accommodation, grooming, regular check-ups, parasite control and vaccination. Most thoroughbreds in training get such a regime and therefore most of them are healthy for most of the time. However they can get viruses, catch other disorders or get injured and worry themselves out of good health.

As you cannot always get to the track, then you have to take it on trust that the horse is fit and well or rely on the TV commentator's observations in this area. *Channel 4 Racing* always give a summary of horses that impressed in the paddock, going to post and those that did not. Checking the last few form ratings can also give you an indication here; have the ratings for last three or four runs been improving or deteriorating? Is there something amiss?

By a well horse we also mean sound in mind as well as body. Some horses look fantastically well but may have serious mind or attitude problems. These horses get a bad name for not doing their best, but you can generally find a reason for their temperamental behaviour because as a rule horses are honest and genuine. There may be some underlying physical weakness that has not been detected by the trainer or the vet. Or as a two year old they may have had a very hard race and never got over it. Whatever the reason or excuse these horses do exist and you need to know how to recognise them and know how to deal with them.

These horses with attitude problems or quirks are sometimes politely known as un-genuine or non-triers or not so politely known as rogues or monkeys. This is not a binary judgement; there are degrees of roguishness. At one end of the scale you will have the inveterate rogue and vagabond who scores ten out of ten for appalling attitude and devilish trickery and on whom you should never risk a sou. At the other end of the scale you have the horse with some small quirk or temporary bad habit that can probably be remedied by blinkers or a visor etc. and that scores only one out of ten.

Always consider the information you have available to you on the attitude of the horse to do its job. Is it genuine or is it a rogue? Some tell-tale signs that a horse may have attitude or other mind problems:

Tail flashing
Not trying and dropping themselves out
Not going through with their effort
Wearing of blinkers, cheekpieces etc. although this is not a reliable sign.

Behaving mulishly, looking reluctant

However the racing press have usually spotted the animals that are not totally enchanted with the sport and generally warn you in the race blurb. **Timeform** will usually point out if a horse is suspected of attitude problems and give it a double squiggle next to its rating if it is confirmed.

Fitness

There are probably two occasions when you need to be sure that a horse is 100% fit. That is upon its first run of the new flat season or its first run after a lay off due to being rested or injured. Before a horse runs how can you evaluate if it is fit or not? There are a couple of ways to tell; the trainer's record and a paddock inspection.

Trainer's record: some trainers have a reputation for having their horses fully fit when they hit the racetrack at the beginning of a new season or after the horse has had a long lay off. Some other trainers bring their horses along more slowly and their charges generally need one or two races to get them fully fit. It is worth getting to know how trainers generally work so you know which horses you can have confidence in first time out.

Paddock inspection: what signs do you look for that will tell you whether a horse is fully fit or not? Look for good muscle definition particularly in the quarters, around the backside. No excess flesh, solid looking, a shiny coat, alert and on its toes. If it is not fully fit it is likely to be carrying condition, looking burly, particularly round the belly, and maybe a little lethargic. And if you can't get to the races and perform a paddock inspection then the experts on *Channel 4 Racing* will usually oblige. Before each televised race they usually highlight the horses that caught the eye in the paddock or going to post, looking fit and well and those who didn't make an impression, looking unfit or off-colour.

The Jockey

I've already touched a little on the importance of jockeyship in the section on pace, but here are a few more pointers on the importance of the man in the saddle making the critical decisions as the race unfolds.

First it is worth looking at what a jockey has to do in a race; he has a number of tasks to perform, the sequence of which is largely dictated by how the race is run:

- Get the horse out of the stalls quickly and secure a good position
- Keep the horse out of trouble
- Take the shortest route
- Find the best ground
- Ride a powerful finish, if still in contention.
- Ride the horse to make best use of its better racing characteristics
- Try to engineer a pace that'll suit their horse
- Be on the lookout for any advantage to themselves and disadvantage to others
- Judge when to go for a gap or make a move to the finish

And all these decisions are made and the actions executed in a split second whilst perched on 1,000 lb of horseflesh travelling at about 35 mph with other horses thundering in front of them, behind them and maybe either side of them, with the other jockeys shouting, waving their whips and manoeuvring their horses. And with thousands of expectant punters roaring them on to boot. Not an easy job by any measure. They deserve our greatest admiration and respect!

To do this demanding job jockeys need to be endowed with a number of special attributes, namely: excellent balance, brains, anticipation, patience, strength, an acute sense of timing, good hands, presence of mind/alertness, flexibility and tactical awareness. Being human all jockeys make mistakes but the main characteristic that separates the really good jockeys from the average is that they make fewer of them. The other is that they are formidable at judging pace.

No jockey can make their horse go faster over a given distance than its natural abilities will allow but they should be able to do most of the above and do them well. Of course nobody is perfect and jockeys, like all of us, have their strengths and weaknesses; which are worth getting to know because in a really open race the man in the saddle can be the main deciding factor.

Talking Tactics
Roy Miller

The top riders make fewer mistakes than the rest

Weight

Weight is a significant factor in determining the outcome of races, particularly handicap races. The majority of races in the UK are handicaps so weight and its effect is a fact of life for most horses and all punters. A horse can continue to win handicap races and each time be penalised by the handicapper with more weight. But in the end there will come a time, perhaps after two, maybe three, even four races when the weight tells and begins to affect the horse's performance. The system will always win in the end, even if it isn't perfect.

Looking for horses that are better than their handicap mark, as previously suggested, pays off because the system is not 100% accurate, more art than science. If a horse is 'well in' at the weights it can often win. Those that are in the 'handicappers grip' will continue to lose until they come down in the weights to a 'winning mark'.

How can you tell if a horse can carry the weight it's allotted in a race?
(See Chapter 2, Pages 27 and 28 plus Chapter 5 page 60 where this question is covered.)

Your research and race reading highlights plus inputs from the Private Handicaps will also tell you which horses are 'well in' at the weights or under-rated.

Question Time For The Also Rans
Roy Miller

There may be a horse in the race that was truly unlucky.
It is probably better that its rating suggests!

Chapter Five

Pulling it all together: The selection and decision-making process

'I used to be indecisive, but now I'm not so sure'
Anon

So how do you pull all the pertinent data together to try to make sense out of a given race and separate those with a chance from the no-hopers? There is an awful lot of data to sieve and to manage in order to extract the precious information. Below is a chart of the key steps in the decision cycle and as you can see there are choices to be made all the way through the process using the information you have gathered and gleaned. Where to locate the necessary information contained within each of these steps was covered in the early chapters, however I will set out in this chapter a quick summary of the key data requirements, along with the necessary actions for assembly and analysis.

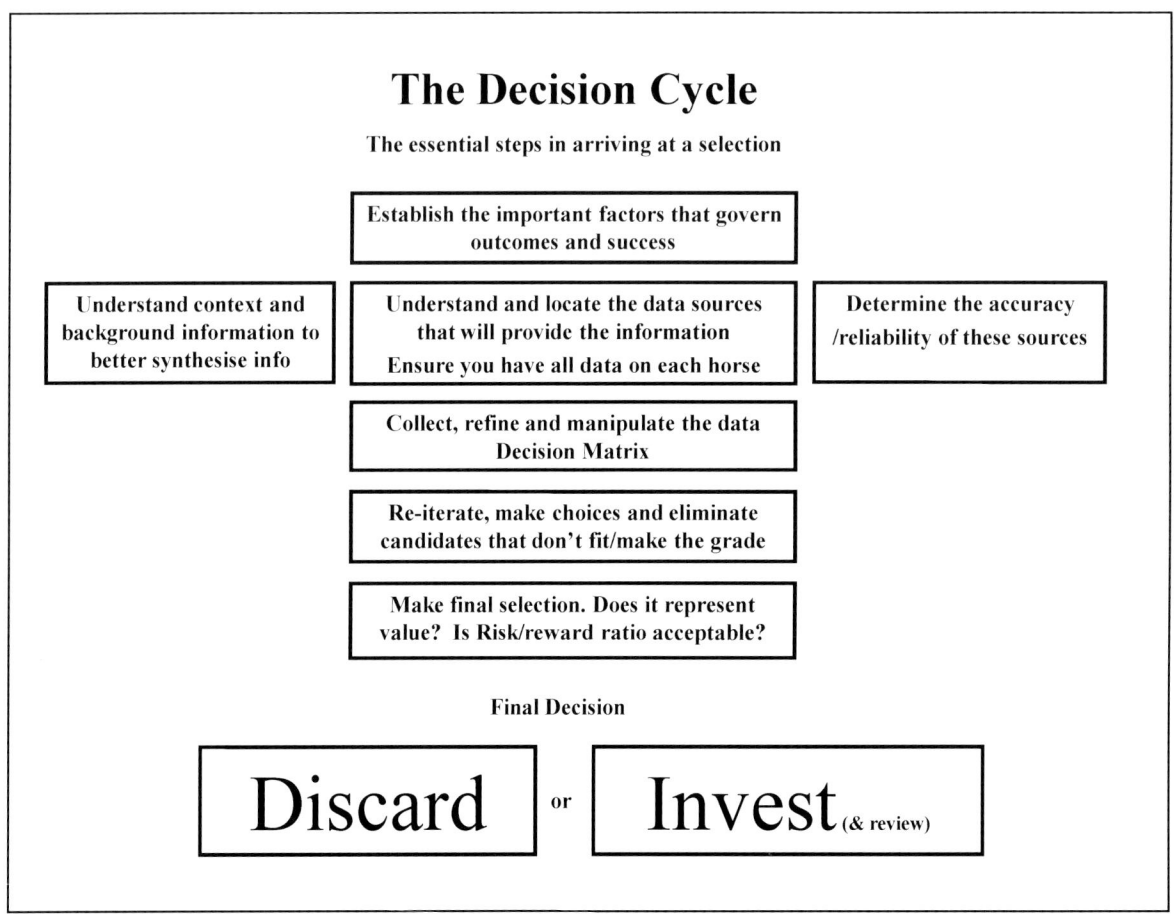

The Decision Cycle

The essential steps in arriving at a selection

| Establish the important factors that govern outcomes and success |

| Understand context and background information to better synthesise info | Understand and locate the data sources that will provide the information. Ensure you have all data on each horse | Determine the accuracy /reliability of these sources |

| Collect, refine and manipulate the data. Decision Matrix |

| Re-iterate, make choices and eliminate candidates that don't fit/make the grade |

| Make final selection. Does it represent value? Is Risk/reward ratio acceptable? |

Final Decision

Discard or Invest (& review)

Step 1: Establish and understand the factors that govern outcomes and success

In any enterprise, if you want to prosper, it's necessary to understand the factors that govern performance and assure successful outcomes. Only then can you profit when you are convinced the principal factors you have identified are all in place. Horse races are no exception. We covered these factors in chapters two, three and four and they are; assessing the basic merit of a horse through both speed and form and by analysing how it will handle the specific race conditions.

However the data containing these governing factors is always mixed in with a mass of other extraneous detail and sometimes it can be difficult to see the wood for the trees. So good selection needs clear thinking; the ability to sort out the essentials from the mass of lesser factors that are available on each and every race. And not only clear thinking but also a resolute focus is necessary to keep the essentials in mind and never lose sight of them and allow the mass of detail to submerge them. So keep it simple and use those factors, and only those factors that are important to outcomes and success.

And remember, you can't make winning decisions without good and adequate performance data on all the horses in a race. No data, or data gaps equals guessing, poor data equals a flawed or bad decision.

Here's a quick summary of the factors that govern outcomes and success of races:

Relative Merits: You can determine the relative merits of each horse in a race by assessing their form and speed. These should be absolutely central to your calculations. The ***form rating*** given to a horse is not an exact science and what you want to find are those horses that are under rated by the official handicapper. You are certainly not interested in those that are over rated. So how do you find those underrated? After each race the official BHA handicapper will review the performance of the principals in a race and, if appropriate, assign them a new form rating or handicap mark. At the same time the private handicappers from ***Timeform, Raceform, The Racing Post*** etc. will do likewise. Although they are all experts at assessing form they will not all agree exactly. Some of the private handicaps will highlight horses that they consider to have been underrated by the official BHA handicapper. It is these under-rated animals you are looking for and it is the private handicaps and/or your observation and research that will hopefully pinpoint them. A good ***speedfigure*** will highlight a horse of promise and ability long before the form lines are all in place. And close scrutiny of the time figures of a compiler you trust will help you pick out these animals.

Race Variables: The important ones are: going, distance, track, (orientation, effect of draw, and access to better ground) jockey, pace, weight carried and fitness/health. How each horse is likely to handle these race variables can de divined from scrutinising their race records; how they cope with certain types of going, a left handed undulating track, which distance they perform best at, etc. The race variables, however, are not absolutes and each one may affect a horse's performance differently, positively or negatively, to varying degrees, some not at all, some a wee bit and some hugely. It is better therefore to weight these factors in your decision making process.

And don't forget the Data: In order to make a good, sensible decision you need adequate data. Data containing sufficient race information on all the above topics. If a given race doesn't throw up sufficient performance information about **all** the runners, if there are gaps, then it is not a good race in which to invest any of your time to seek a betting opportunity. It will be a race best observed. At one end of the scale you will have 2 year old maiden stakes where all the runners have never raced before so there is zero information about their merit or their racing characteristics. Then you may have the 3-year-old maiden stakes where there is some (not much) information about many of the runner and zero information about a few. And at the other end of the scale you will have the all age handicap or group races where there is information aplenty about all the runners. Be highly selective about which races you choose to analyse never mind invest in. If there is little or no data available about a given race then at best observe and at worst ignore!

Step 2: Understand and locate the main data sources.

When compiling speed and form performance figures for flat horses racing in the UK, you need two other important ingredients: lots of time and plenty of expertise. As most of us are short of one, or both of these, I suggest it is better to consult the private handicaps. There are several good ones around, *Timeform, Raceform Update, The Weekender, Racing Post (Postdata* for form *Topspeed* for speed*)* and they are very reliable and dependable**.** You needn't consult them all, maybe two or three at most; choose the ones you feel most comfortable with. Both form and speed are usually contained within one source. When starting out test each publication in turn and then decide which one you feel is the better. Not only in terms of accuracy of data provided but also clarity of layout, presentation, ease of use etc.

Locating the data on how each horse will most likely handle the race variables can be a little more time consuming. Most of this data will be found and can be assessed by referring to the form section in the **Racing Post** or the **Raceform Update** or similar publications. These are 100% accurate historical records of each horse's racing history and with careful attention you can tell what a horse's preferences are for going, distance, track orientation etc. (see examples of **Wigwam Willie** and **Generous Jem** in the form summaries section in chapter two.) The exception is, of course, fitness and well-being. For this you have to rely on either the trainer's track record for producing horses race-fit or, more importantly, by casting a critical eye over the animal in the paddock or as it canters down to post and then making your own decision about its fitness and well-being.

Step 2a: Determine the accuracy/reliability of the sources

The available data that tells you how good a horse is and how it runs its races falls into two categories and each needs to be treated differently. First is the historical 100% purely factual data, which you need to interpret in order to divine how a horse will handle the race variables. This base, raw data, given reasonable interpretation by yourself, should give you pointers about a horse's likely performance, under certain conditions, such as track, going, distance etc. The second type of data is that already calculated and interpreted by 'experts' regarding form and speed and can vary somewhat in accuracy and reliability depending upon your source.

Historical data needs sensible interpretation by you to gain an insight into how each horse is likely to handle the race conditions or the race variables. Data from the industry 'experts' on form or speed requires you to select which of the expert's calculations are the more accurate and reliable.

Race Variables

The horse's form record is 100% factual and will give you accurate historical information. It will tell you how a horse ran during its last few races; the track, the distance, the going, the jockey, the time the race was run in and the position the horse finished. It will also tell you the horse's current BHA rating, how many runs the horse has had, how many wins at what rating, at what distance and on what going. That is all the record will tell you; it is completely neutral and factual. It's up to you what you make of it. Everyone has access to this data so it's the quality of your interpretation that can make the difference. You will have to read this data and make some decisions about each horse involved in a particular race. From what you have surmised about a certain horse's past performances you will then have to ask yourself a number of questions as you seek to interpret the data. Can this horse stay the distance of this race? Will it handle the going and the track? Will it have a chance off its current rating (at these weights)? Will it be fit? You might find a horse that is, according to speed and form figures, not the best in the race but your interpretation of the historical data tells you it will most probably handle the race conditions much better than the rest. This is really a test of how well you can interpret the data and this is a mixture of experience and knowledge (see page 27).

Establishing the Merit of a Horse

The private handicap form ratings and the speedfigures are a very different kettle of fish. Producing them is not an exact science. They are 'expert' opinions based on close race observation for the form rating and complicated calculations founded on race times for the speedfigures. The resulting 'expert' output can vary in accuracy and reliability. As there is only one race winner, some will be very much more accurate than others and you will soon spot the reliable and accurate ones.

Form: The official handicapper is responsible for giving a horse a form rating or handicap mark; this will determine what weight a horse will carry in its races. However giving a horse a form rating is largely subjective. Each private handicapper will read a race differently from the official handicapper and have their own opinion of how well each horse in the race performed. Therefore the private handicaps will differ, in some instances, from the official handicap. It is the horses that the private handicapper highlights as being, in his or her opinion, under-rated or 'well in' at the weights that are worth a second look and further scrutiny.

Speedfigures: If you examine the output of different compilers of speedfigures you will find differences in their interpretation of how fast a certain horse ran in a given race. This is because each compiler probably uses a slightly different equation when working out their figures. Each one uses a calculation for turning a race time into a speedfigure that has been adapted and modified over the years as a result of learning and personal experience. Nuances they have picked up from certain tracks, certain types of going, wind directions etc. that demand small adjustments to their speed workings. And, no doubt, each one of them thinks their speedfigures are the most accurate and reliable. You will be the best judge of that.

Initially it is worth working with a variety of private handicaps and speed rating compilers to see whose output you prefer. You will probably find that some are better at rating two year olds, some at all-age handicaps and some at pattern races. Horses for courses really!

Step 2b: Understand the Context

If you understand a subject reasonably well you can usually interpret any additional information you receive concerning it quite competently. Information received, when you don't have much background information on the subject at hand, can often be puzzling and quite meaningless. As a schoolboy, like me, you were probably crammed with information, which you had to regurgitate in order to pass exams. Comprehension was not a priority, you knew it but didn't completely understand it. However in later life you probably, again like me, have experienced profound 'Ah! Ah!' moments. These are instances where, as you became more familiar with a subject, you were able to piece together bits of information that had before seemed irrelevant and completely unconnected. Suddenly you are then presented with blinding insights that before have eluded you, as most of the data you were being fed was out of context. Context is important.

For example breeding can be important in helping you answer some difficult questions particularly about the distance a younger horse may stay when there is no definitive race data.

So in order to rely on your own judgements read around the subject, in the short term it may seem pointless but, believe me, in the long run it will pay off. It will help you to synthesise the information better and make more accurate decisions.

Step 3: Collect, Refine and Manipulate the Data

When you have located your main data sources and evaluated the accuracy and reliability of them you can begin to pull together the pertinent information contained therein. I'm not smart enough to hold all the data in my head so I much prefer to analyse the available information on a simple chart. I find it is much easier and more efficient to process and interpret the data working with a matrix. It is best to keep it as simple as possible and assembled on one page. Set out on the next page is a matrix that you might want to begin with; you can always develop or adapt it to suit yourself as you gain more confidence and experience.

The Decision Matrix

Form and Speed: are the key indicators of the merit of a horse. Assessing these factors will highlight the key players in a race. First, enter the data from your preferred private handicap(s) and from this you can then develop a short list of perhaps four or five horses that are worthy of further analysis. Then take closer look at them and assess how these likely principal players will cope with the race variables.

The decision matrix with form and speedfigures entered to establish a short list

The Decision Matrix

Horse	Form	Speed	dist	going	track	fitness	pace	weight	jockey	Short list
1 Bounding Bertie	95	105								
2 The Rocket	93	101								
3 Amble Along	97	109								
4 Pedestrian	90	89								
5 Zipper	87	97								
6 Bumble	95	103								
7 Shifter	83	96								
8 Zoom Zoom	83	90								
9 Dawdle	81	92								
10 Hang About	80	94								
Establish the relative merits of each horse in race			**Analyse how each horse is likely to handle the race variables**							

12 Furlongs, heavy going, York

Deciding on the short list

In the above chart the form and speedfigures have been filled in from a private handicap to establish the principal players and to determine a short list for further analysis. **Bounding Bertie, The Rocket, Amble Along** and **Bumble** all have good form and speedfigures and present themselves for further analysis. **Pedestrian** has reasonable form and a borderline speedfigure, whilst **Zipper** has reasonable form and a goodish speedfigure. The first four horses should go on the short list, no doubt. The last two, are borderline. For the final analysis against race variables I will leave them off the short list in my example. As a rule of thumb, I normally put somewhere between a third to half of the runners on my list for further inspection, depending upon how competitive the race is. So putting four out of ten on the list here feels about right. However, when starting out, you may wish to include a couple more on your short-list to get practice.

Race Variables: When you have produced a short list, determined by the speed and form figures, then rate the candidates against the race variables in order to help you locate the likely winner. I mentioned earlier that these race variables are not binary; with each one it's a question of degree so it is well worth weighting the scores here. For example:

Will the horse get the distance? If you are absolutely positive the horse in question can perform well over the distance in question; for example if it is already a distance winner, then score it a perfect ten. If there is a small niggley doubt about stamina then score it a seven or eight. If you cannot fathom it at all give it a five and if you are 100% positive that the trip is either too far or too short score it a zero. Remember if a horse has not competed over this distance before its breeding can sometimes be a useful guide.

Will the horse act on the going? If the horse has already won on this going you can score a ten. If it has run with merit without winning perhaps getting in the frame, then score it a seven or eight. If its record suggests it won't handle the going at all well then score it low, a two or a three at best. Extremes of going can prove difficult for a lot of horses, a select few can handle them and not many at all relish them!

Will the horse handle the track? Don't forget there are a couple of factors at work here: either the course orientation (left handed/right handed) or the effect of the draw (shortest route and/or access to better ground). This is your judgement on the day and again worth weighting as above. If a horse is already a course winner this will help in weighting your score.

Is the horse fit/healthy? When a horse is appearing for the first time that season, after a long lay off or after an unaccountably bad performance last time, these fitness and health factors are worth close analysis. All the race variables can be checked out by desk research *except* fitness and well-being where, I'm afraid, there is really no good substitute for a paddock inspection. However some trainers have a good reputation for turning out their horses ready to perform after a long lay-off. On the other hand some are renowned for not having them quite ready and who need a race to get them 100% fit. If the horse you are interested in has had a long lay off research the trainer record/reputation in this area and score them accordingly.

Will the horse appreciate the likely pace? How the race will be run is important to the outcome but devilishly difficult to predict. All you can do is try to ascertain what sort of pace would suit the animal you are interested in and by looking at the participants try to predict who will make the running and what sort of pace would be likely. If it's a valuable race or a big field it is more than likely the pace will be true.

Will the horse comfortably carry the allotted weight? The first decision is to have it clear in your own mind if the animal in question:

a) is improving
b) has plateaued
c) is regressing.

This will help you deal more effectively with the available data and decide what to do. Lets say, for example, a given horse has won four times, being rated 68, 71, 73 and 78. For the upcoming race, this horse in question is now rated 83, that is 5lb more than its highest winning rating. If it is still improving there is a very good chance it could score again if all other race factors are in its favour. If it has plateaued then there is not much likelihood of it winning unless it has a good apprentice on board claiming 5 or 7 lb. And if it is regressing then you could discount it altogether from your calculations. So if it is improving you could rate it somewhere twixt eight and ten. If it has plateaued it's a low score unless there is a claimer aboard. And finally if it's regressing it should score zero.

A good way of gathering the pertinent data that will tell you if a horse is progressing or regressing is to look at the *Timeform* rating summary (covered on page 24) or consult the *Racing Post* form summary (covered on pages 27-28)

How competent is the jockey? Most professional jockeys are highly competent and if the horse is a straightforward ride you can safely rate most a ten. If the horse has the services of a claimer then you might want to deduct a point or two. If a horse is a known 'difficult' ride, needs producing late, or needs to make all the running etc., then it is worth concentrating on the strengths and weakness of the jockey concerned; whether they have ridden the horse in question before and scoring them accordingly.

Example: The decision matrix filled in

The Decision Matrix

Horse	Form	Speed	dist	going	track	fitness	pace	weight	jockey	Short list
1 Bounding Bertie	95	105	10	10	8	8	10	5	10	(61)
2 The Rocket	93	101	8	4	10	10	8	5	10	(57)
3 Amble Along	97	109	10	10	10	8	10	8	8	(64)
4 Pedestrian	90	89								
5 Zipper	87	97								
6 Bumble	95	103	7	10	10	8	10	10	8	(63)
7 Shifter	83	96								
8 Zoom Zoom	83	90								
9 Dawdle	81	92								
10 Hang About	80	94								
Establish the relative merits of each horse in race			Analyse how each horse is likely to handle the race variables							

When you have scored your principals against the variables and added up the scores then go back over the figures. Analyses critically the horses on the short list; which looks the best? Do any of the low scores appear to be showstoppers? Such as extremes of going (which many horses can't handle), carrying more weight than ever before (but with no answers to it like rapid improvement or a claiming jockey, etc.)

Bounding Bertie scores very low on weight as he is on a handicap mark seven points (lb) higher than he has ever won before. He does not have a claimer on board to negate this and it is a worry particularly as he is a six year old and has most likely plateaued. This race is unknown territory for him. **The Rocket** has never won (or run well) on this going and it is a big question mark, hence the low score of four. It is also on a rating seven points higher than it has ever won at, so it is carrying two big question marks! **Amble Along** looks good on most variables; its lowest scores of eight on fitness, weight and jockey can be easily explained. Being off the track for five weeks isn't that long and anyway its trainer has an excellent record of preparing her horses well. It is on a mark two points higher than ever before but has an excellent 3lb claiming jockey aboard. **Bumble** scores low on distance, as it has never won, or run well, over this trip before. There are slight concerns over both fitness and jockey, as it has been off the track for six weeks and has a claiming jockey on board.

On first review **Amble Along** looks very good, as it is six points ahead on speed and with no really serious concerns or showstoppers regarding the variables. **Bumble** could also be a contender, if you satisfy yourself that it can stay the distance.

Step 4: Re-iterate and make choices

After your first review it is worth going over the runners again, this time with a super critical eye to make sure you have not taken any of the data at face value, or missed anything of significance. Go over all the runners again, there may be a young, well rated horse in the line up that has improved by three or four lb on each of its last few runs and so is very much on the upgrade and may be worth much closer inspection, even promotion to the short list. Double check how each horse achieved its ratings, both form and speed. Review each horse's likes and dislikes with regard to race variables to ensure you have not missed anything and you have scored each accurately. Double check that there are no showstoppers in the variables for your short listed horses.

Step 5: Make the final selection

In 80 or 90% of cases the review should confirm the horse that looked the best from the short list. However if the review highlights another horse then compare that one with your original leading contender once more against the main decision criteria. If it is a rapid improver then add the points by which you think it will improve to its score when you do the final comparison. Then make your choice.

Step 6: Discard or Invest

Having analysed all the horses in a given race you should get a very good feel about the openness of the race and the chances of your final selection. You should be able to gauge whether the horse has a very strong chance or whether the race is really wide open. Also the odds available for the horse in question will help in your final decision. If the horse has a very strong chance and there is 'value' in the odds available then invest. If you feel the race is open and/or there is not much value in the odds available then either wager a small amount or discard and move onto the next opportunity.

& Review

After you have invested always review the result, win or lose. This is where you can learn some invaluable lessons. What was it about your selection that worked or what vital clue did you miss regarding the winner? This way you build up knowledge and expertise and better understand the key points to look for in a winning selection.

Giants Causeway
Roy Miller

He was a very tough horse, never knew when he was beaten

Conclusion

'If you always do what you always did then you'll always get what you always got'
Anon

Racing can be quite complex; the handicapping system, the types of races and the conditions attached, the quantity of data on form, speed and race variables produced, etc., can really make the temples throb. Therefore, in this book, I have omitted any extraneous material and tried to keep it as simple and as focussed as possible, concentrating only on the essentials. Again, in the interests of simplicity, I have restricted this book to the flat although the principles covered are also applicable to National Hunt.

I hope you have found the approach I've outlined useful and instructive in determining a horse's merit and analysing whether its racing characteristics will suit the prevailing race conditions. And that you have also found some of the hints and tips I've included for selection and betting make good sense and are of practical value. It is quite a rigorous approach but I'm positive that the results will help you derive much more interest and satisfaction from your involvement.

Finally, I would like to leave you with these thoughts:

- You can't select winners without all the appropriate data on each and every horse in a race.
- The information you pull together on a race is seldom 100% self-explanatory and will need your analysis. Weeding out the no hopers is quite simple; trying to separate the two or three main contenders is quite difficult.
- Always keep in mind the essentials that determine success and outcomes (form, speed, variables) and nothing else.
- Bet only when everything is in your favour and there is 'value' to be found in the available odds.
- Don't trust systems, tipsters or 'inside information.' Trust only yourself!
- Have fun and enjoy yourself.

So, in future, why don't you try something different; you never know it might just work!

Good luck!

Glossary of Terms

A

Apprentices: trainee jockeys, sometimes know as claimers, who receive a weight allowance in a race to compensate for their lack of experience. Initially an apprentice can claim 7lb in a race, this decreases to 5lb after 20 wins, to 3lb after 50 wins; the apprentice loses the claim entirely after 95 wins and then must compete against all other professional jockeys on an equal basis. If a horse was set to carry 9st.0lb in a handicap race but had the services of a 7lb claimer, the horse would carry 8st.7lb. Claimers or apprentices cannot ride in group races.

Aqueduct: a racecourse in New York City

B

Bay: one of the colours of a thoroughbred racehorse. The bay has a dark brown coat turning to black on the lower legs. It also has a black tail and mane.

Bay Meadows: a racecourse in San Francisco, California.

Better Ground: the most suitable racing surface on a racetrack. Before racing a jockey or trainer may walk the course to see where the *'better ground'* lies and steer their mount there during the race in order to gain an edge on the other runners. Because of the weather, track usage, watering systems, track drainage etc., the *'better ground'* can, and does, move.

Beyer: he is the most widely used compiler of racehorse speedfigures in the USA. These are printed in the **Daily Raceform** and are known as the *'Beyer Figures'*

Bit: a piece of ironmongery that fits into the horse's mouth and is attached to the reins. Early in the race a horse will be tightly held or restrained by the jockey to conserve its energy and it will be pulling on the bit. The horse is then (because it is still running well within itself) 'on the bit'. Later in the race, near the finish, when the jockey lets the horse go, (and the horse is flat out and not pulling on the bit) it is then 'off the bit'. When a horse 'comes off the bit' early in a race it often means it is struggling to cope with the speed or the distance. And of course the last horse to 'come off the bit' usually wins. ('On the bridle' and 'off the bridle' mean exactly the same thing)

Blinkers: headwear for the horse that restricts its peripheral vision, allowing it only to look straight ahead. These are fitted to help the horse concentrate on the job of running and hopefully improve its performance

British Horseracing Authority: the current governing body for horse racing in the United Kingdom.

Brown: one of the colours of a thoroughbred racehorse. The coat (including mane and tail) is very dark brown almost black.

C

Canter: the gait of a horse between a trot and a gallop

Cheek pieces: headwear for the horse to restrict vision and help it concentrate. They are two strips of sheepskin fastened to each side of the horse's head, attached to the bridle. They are far less restricting than blinkers or visors.

Chestnut: one of the colours of a thoroughbred racehorse. The chestnut has a golden brown coat varying from light to dark (Liver chestnut). The mane and tail are also of the same colour

Classic Race: the five 'classic' races are: The 2,000 Guineas, The Derby, The St Leger, The 1,000 Guineas and The Oaks. The 'Triple Crown': The 2000 Guineas, The Derby and The St Leger.

Colt: a male horse under the age of five.

D

Dam: the female parent of a horse.

Derby: is a Group 1 race for 3 year olds run over 12 furlongs at Epsom racecourse in early June and is the second classic race of the season.

Draw: the random choice of how horses will line up to start a race. At a number of racecourses the draw can confer certain advantages on some horses; for example better ground or a shorter route to the finish.

F

Falsely run: a race is described as being *'falsely run'* when a slow pace prevails and can often cause a surprise result. The resulting form can therefore be suspect.

Filly: a female horse under the age of five.

Form: the race history of a thoroughbred racehorse that gives a very good indication of its class or merit.

Fully wound up: a 100% fit horse.

Furlong: horse races are measured in furlongs. There are eight furlongs in a mile.

G

Gallop: the fastest gait of a horse

Gallops: the gallops are the grounds where trainers run their horses to get them fit.

Gelding: a castrated male horse

Going: 'the going' is the current state of the ground on a racecourse. Going varies from hard, firm, good to firm, good, good to soft, soft and heavy; depending upon how much moisture there is in the ground.

Grey: one of the colours of a thoroughbred racehorse. The coat contains both black and white hairs and it lightens with age, becoming almost white.

Group Races: these are the highest class of races. There are four grades of race in this class. Starting with horses rated 110 plus and are, in ascending order of class and importance; Listed, Group 3, Group 2 and Group 1

H

Hand: a unit of length equalling four inches used for measuring the height of horses. Thoroughbred racehorses are usually between 15 and 17 hands high (to the shoulder).

Handicaps: are types of race where each horse carries a different weight according to its official BHA handicap mark. This weight differential is to equalise each horse's chance of winning and to make the races more exciting and competitive. One point is equal to 1lb.

Handicap Mark: each horse's ability is expressed in a number or handicap mark. These handicap marks are allotted by the official BHA handicapper on a 0 to 130+ scale, the higher the number the better the horse. Also the higher the number the more weight a horse will carry in a race. This rating or handicap mark is revised each time a horse runs by the official handicapper; upwards by a few points if it wins or gets in the frame and downwards if it loses. A horse's handicap mark is its entry ticket to a specific grade of race.

Handicapper: a horse that participates in handicap races or a person who awards horses a 'handicap mark' either officially or privately.

Hobby: a breed of horse indigenous to the British Isles. It was bred with Arabian and Barb bloodstock in the eighteenth century to produce the thoroughbred and was the source of speed in the breed.

Horse: a male horse aged five or over.

I

In the frame: horses that take the first 3 places in a race are 'in the frame' or have 'made the frame' (except in a handicap race with 16+ runners when the first 4 places are 'in the frame')

J

Jockey Club: an organisation that was formed in the mid eighteenth century and from that time and until quite recently, governed and regulated racing in the UK. An un-elected body based in Newmarket, its members are mainly aristocratic. The club is not open for membership you must be invited to join. Exclusive. Now subsumed within the BHA.

K

Kentucky: a state of the USA and the major centre for racehorse breeding there.

L

Listed Race: the lowest grade of class 1 or group races

M

Mare: a female horse aged five or over

Maiden: a horse that has not won a race

Maiden Race: is for horses that have not won a race

Make the running: the horse that leads the field early in a race and by 'making the running' it has a major influence on the speed, or pace, at which the race is run.

N

Nap: the strongest prediction a tipster makes.

Nursery Handicap: a handicap race for two year olds

O

Orientation: racecourses in the UK have either a left-handed or right-handed orientation; or if you prefer, clockwise and anti-clockwise. Unlike the courses in the USA, which are all, anti-clockwise or left handed.

P

Pace: the rate or speed at which a race is run.

Pacemaker: the horse that leads the field in the early stages of a race thereby determining the pace. In valuable races some owners will run two horses, one of which will be the pacemaker in order to ensure a strong and genuine pace. This tactic helps in assuring that the best horse will win.

Paddock: on the racecourse this is another name for the parade-ring where the public can inspect the horses before the race.

Palomino: one of the colours of a thoroughbred racehorse. The palomino has a golden coloured coat and a cream almost white tail and mane.

Pattern Races: another name for group one, two and three races.

Pedigree: all thoroughbred racehorses are pedigree and their ancestry can be traced, to the origin of the breed, through the 'Stud Book'.

Private Handicap: as opposed to the official handicap produced by the BHA. As rating a horse is not an exact science parallel rating systems have been developed notably by *Timeform* and *Raceform*: Their main aim is to highlight horses that are better than the official handicap suggests and therefore well weighted.

R

Raceform: an organisation based in Newbury, Berkshire, that, amongst other things, publishes the revised changes to the official handicap marks from the previous week's UK racing in its weekly publication the *Raceform Update*. The weekly *Update* also contains the race cards for all races in the UK from Wednesday to Sunday and included on these cards are their private handicap ratings and speedfigures. All the previous week's UK results are to be found here too along with all European pattern races.

Racing Post: A daily publication and the industry's newspaper. It contains all the daily race cards and the form of all runners. It also includes the 5-day entries and the 48-hour declarations. The race cards also contain their private handicap and speedfigures. Accompanying the cards is expert analysis and commentary.

Roan: one of the colours of a thoroughbred racehorse. The coat can be bay, (red roan) chestnut (strawberry roan) or black/brown (blue roan) and in each case the coat is sprinkled with white hairs. As the horse ages it becomes increasingly more white.

S

Selling Plater: a lowly rated horse of little merit.

Sire: the father of a racehorse

Sloppy: in the USA the normal racing surface is dirt and when it is very wet the going becomes 'sloppy'.

Stallion: a male horse, usually standing at stud.

Standard: the normal state of going on all weather or dirt tracks.

Standard Times: in order to compile accurate speedfigures it is necessary to establish the average or standard time necessary to run all the race distances advertised at every British racetrack. This is necessary because all courses are different. For example the running of 6 furlongs at Epsom is about 5 seconds faster than 6 furlongs at Pontefract. *Raceform* publish their course standard times regularly in their weekly *Raceform Update.*

Stewards: the judges that officiate at a racecourse

St Leger: is the third classic race of the season run over 14 furlongs at Doncaster in September.

T

Tattersalls: an enclosure for the public at racecourses in the UK. Named after Richard Tattersall, founder of a famous horse market in London and owner of the famous racehorse ***Highflyer***

Thoroughbred: a breed of horse specifically developed for racing. Originating in England in the late seventeenth and early eighteenth centuries

Timeform: an organisation that produces racing commentaries, in particular race cards for all meetings containing their private handicap and speed figures. It was founded by Phil Bull in the late 1940's and is based in Halifax, Yorkshire.

Tote (Pari-Mutuel): *Tote* or *Pari-Mutuel* systems operate by pooling all bets on a particular race and sharing the proceeds amongst the winners. Punters are competing against other punters rather than against the book. *Tote or Pari-Mutuel* systems are usually owned and operated by National Racing Authorities and the profits are ploughed back into the sport.

Two Thousand Guineas: is the first classic race of the season. It is for three year olds and is run over a mile at Newmarket racecourse early in May.

V

Visor: headgear for horses to help them concentrate on running. Similar to blinkers but not as restricting

W

Well in at the weights: a favourably handicapped horse is well in at the weights.

Withers: the highest part of the back of a horse, behind the neck between the shoulders

BIBLIOGRAPHY

Wright H.	*Bull The Biography*	1995
Leach J.	*Sods I have cut on the* Turf	1961
Leach J.	*A Rider in the Stand*	1970
Rodrigo R.	*The Paddock Book*	1967

10 WINNING WAYS   3 8-4   (visor) **118** p

b.f. Alzao (USA) 117 – Sweet Talking 82 (Sharpen Up 127) [2003 7m^b a6g^2 :: 2004 7s* 8f 8d* May 1]
IR 12,500Y: compact filly: half-sister to several winners, including useful miler Chatterbox (by
Formidable): dam 6f winner: quickened well to win maiden at Thirsk in April and handicap at
Newmarket in May: stays 1m: acts on soft going, probably unsuited by firm: visored this year:
improving and should win more races when conditions are favourable. (114Nm8d 91Th7s 72'Li6g)
M. JOHNSTON   K. Darley drawn 12
Black, white epaulets, black and white quartered cap (Timeform Social Club)

		88
8d	118	81
8f	95	83A
7s	116	M
a6g'	106	W
7m'	89 +	M

USING THE TIMEFORM RACE CARD

The RATINGS (expressed in pounds) indicate, at today's weights, the chances of the runners based on Timeform's interpretation of their form. Timeform Ratings on their own should never be taken as indicating a selection; a relatively low rating indicates the amount of improvement the horse will probably have to show and the commentaries may suggest circumstances in which it could find that improvement. The ratings are adjusted for Timeform weight-for-age (the TWFA is given under the race title) and to 10-0 (12-0 for amateurs events). Provisional ratings for newcomers in some maiden and conditions events appear in square brackets and are directly comparable.

For out-of-form horses rated ? adjusted ratings appear for information in the summary.

p the horse is likely to improve   + the horse may be better than rated

P the horse is capable of *much* better   § the horse is unreliable (for temperamental or other reasons)

? the rating is suspect or (used alone) the horse is out of form or can't be assessed with confidence

§§ the horse is so unsatisfactory as to be not worth a rating

Horses which have shown improved form on an artificial surface are either rated on their lower turf form (perhaps with a +) when they return to turf or, when we are confident they may well be better than when last running on turf, on their higher artificial surface form. Some horses with turf form may appear with a ? when they run on an artificial surface for the first time.

The RATINGS SUMMARY indicates, also at today's weights, how each runner with a Timeform Rating has performed in up to its last six races (most recent first, some foreign races may not appear).

The COMMENTARIES contain a wealth of valuable information about each horse's record, what sort of form it is in, ground and distance requirements, temperamental characteristics, favoured tactics, etc. Certain pieces of information appear if we think it is of relevance to the punter. These include bandages, boots, severe nosebands, tongue ties, early to post, etc.

continued inside back cover ...

Front cover photo by Bill Selwyn: Islington (Kieren Fallon)

continued from inside front cover

GUIDE TO ABBREVIATIONS

FORM SUMMARIES: These list a horse's performances in sequence, showing, for each race, its distance in furlongs, the state of the going (as returned by Timeform) and the horse's placing (* denotes a win) if in the first six at the finish. The prefix 'a' signifies a race run on an artificial surface, except 'f' for fibresand at Southwell and Wolverhampton and 'p' for polytrack at Lingfield. Sometimes indicated are wo-walkover, dis-disqualified, rtr-refused to race. The date of the most recent race is included.

The **GOING:** f firm (or fast), m good to firm, g good (or standard), d good to soft or dead, s soft (slow, sloppy or muddy), v heavy

RATINGS SUMMARY: In the third column, where the BHB or Irish Turf Club mark appears if the race is a handicap, the following may also appear:

> G1 Group/Grade 1, G2 Group/Grade 2, G3 Group/Grade 3, L Listed, W Weight-for-age/minor events/classified stakes etc, M Maiden, N Nursery, S Seller, C Claiming event, A Amateur, apprentice, ladies event, etc.

One of two symbols may appear with the Timeform individual performance figures:

> + the performance may be better than rated, or the horse has been rated value more than the bare form

> ? the performance may not be worth the rating shown, or the rating is suspect.

TIMEFIGURES: Timefigures (printed at the end of the commentary measure the performances of horses in terms of race times. Generally speaking, the more recent a horse's good timefigure, the greater its significance and reference to it will be deleted after a horse has run ten times subsequently. *Note: Timefigures recorded at all-weather meetings appear on the cards for all-weather meetings only, in italics to distinguish them from those on turf.*

125'As12m signifies an adjusted timefigure of 125 recorded at Ascot over 12 furlongs on good to firm going. The tick after the 125 signifies last season.

Track abbreviations: The first two letters of a course's name are used in most cases. Note should be made of Bv-Beverley; Ch-Chester; Cp-Chepstow; Ct-Catterick; Ha-Haydock; Hm-Hamilton; Nb-Newbury; Nc-Newcastle; Nm-Newmarket; Sa-Sandown; Sb-Salisbury.

JOCKEYS: Overweight carried should always be deducted from the race rating (but please note that Timeform advertising statements are based upon the ratings given on the card). *Note: Jockeys on this Card are those that were declared at the time of going to press. Some of the riding arrangements may have changed.*

The **DRAW** sometimes has considerable importance, and, if so, advice to that effect will appear in the notes below the racecourse diagram.

The **TRW FIGURES** (printed above the title of some non-handicap races) are the weight-adjusted TIMEFORM RATINGS which the WINNERS have achieved in the same race in the five previous years, the most recent being to the right before the average. A horse with a rating or timefigure better than the TRW figures should be considered seriously.

Please note that the timings of some races at the televised meetings may be subject to change. Details are announced the day before on BBC Ceefax, page 691.

ACKNOWLEDGEMENTS

I am hugely indebted to the following people and organisations without whose help and cooperation this book could not have been written:

The *Timeform* Organisation and Geoff Greetham, for their help and cooperation and for allowing me to reproduce examples from their private handicap that illustrate and explain many points in this book.

Raceform and the editor Bernie Ford, for their help and cooperation, and for allowing me to reproduce examples of their private handicap featured in the ***Raceform Update***.

The ***Racing Post*** and Chris Smith the editor, for their assistance and cooperation in allowing me to feature examples of their race cards and form summaries.

To Stella Robertson, for her patience and good humour in testing the drafts to ensure they were readable and comprehensible.

To Roy Miller, who kindly allowed me to reproduce some of his beautiful paintings to illustrate the book.

To Roger and Elizabeth Bagnall, for their patience and their time in reading the drafts and suggesting corrections and improvements.

To Roger Cousins, for taking the time and trouble to read the drafts and make sensible amendments.

To David Wilkinson, for his most practical help and advice on writing and publishing a book.

To my racing chum Michael Gibbs, for his encouragement and his invaluable feedback to the drafts I produced of this book. Also for the sentiments expressed in the foreword, which are very much appreciated.

To my partner Lorna whose love, patience and encouragement kept me motivated and kept me going. Without her technical help and interventions I would have been reduced to a gibbering pile of rubble.

So many thanks to you all from a most appreciative author.